Deares
Love & Hugs!
Grammy

I Wish Someone
Had Told Me...

ALSO BY DANA PERINO

Everything Will Be Okay

Let Me Tell You About Jasper

And the Good News Is . . .

I Wish Someone Had Told Me …

The Best Advice for Building a Great
Career and a Meaningful Life

Dana Perino

HarperCollins books may be purchased for educational, business, or sales promotional use. For information, please email the Special Markets Department at SPsales@harpercollins.com.

Fox News Books imprint and logo are trademarks of Fox News Network LLC.

FIRST EDITION

Designed by Michele Cameron

Library of Congress Cataloging-in-Publication Data has been applied for.

ISBN 978-0-06-341147-0

25 26 27 28 29 LBC 5 4 3 2 1

To my husband, Peter McMahon

Contents

Introduction

Quick—what's the best advice you ever got?

The advice that made the biggest difference to you and that you pass on the most?

Go ahead and think about it, we've got time. I'm in no hurry. This is your life we're talking about.

I'll ask myself the same question. I'm tempted to give 1,422 different answers (I've asked for a lot of advice!).

So, if I had to choose just one—it would be this:

"Do not pass up the chance to be loved."

It was 1997. I was twenty-five years old. I remember it like it was two hours ago. It changed my life.

I had fallen in love on a plane with a man randomly seated next to me on a flight from Denver to Chicago. We talked for two and a half hours. I was completely charmed— excited and calm at the same time. I felt fully like myself in his presence. And I worried I'd never see him again.

What I didn't know is he felt the same way. We had a whirlwind long-distance romance. Long-form written letters (sent with a stamp!), several trips across the Atlantic for weekends that flew by, afternoons browsing together at bookshops. I was in heaven.

A couple of months later, we were together at a holiday gathering in Denver. I told a good family friend that I was unsure what was next for us. I feared what people would think about our age difference (Peter says he's always liked older women . . . yet I was eighteen years *younger* than him). And the fact that I would have to leave my job on Capitol Hill to move to England to be with him. I couldn't work when I got there because I didn't have a visa (these things mattered then and I'm nothing if not law-abiding).

There were a dozen reasons why this wasn't going to work, but then my friend Kim Wilkerson said, "Stop. Do not pass up the chance to be loved."

She said exactly what I needed to hear. It was the best advice and led to the chance to build a wonderful life with this crazy Brit I've called my husband for twenty-six years.

When I met Peter, I had not been the White House press secretary, cohost of a hit show on Fox News, or the mom to the three Vizslas we've raised together. Without him, none of that would have mattered as much. And probably wouldn't have happened anyway. These life journeys we're on give us countless opportunities to make choices—and to make the most of the outcomes.

Every experience in my life came with a lesson and maybe a little wisdom/advice to impart. I've been lucky— I've gotten great advice along the way from a president, cabinet secretaries, journalists and commentators, officers in the military, members of Congress, and a wonderful peer group of professional men and women with similar career challenges.

Over the years I've gotten a lot of joy from mentoring younger people. I started Minute Mentoring with friends after my White House years, and then included my best mentoring advice in *And the Good News Is* and *Everything Will Be Okay*. I leaned toward mentoring young women in my writing, but I have realized how men too have questions and need support as they navigate their careers. This book is my attempt to put it all together for *everyone*.

When my mom read *Everything Will Be Okay*, she said, "I wish someone had told me these things."

She said that when she entered the workforce in the 1960s . . . well, workplaces were very different then. Opportunities for women were limited. There was no mentor-match program back then. You were on your own. But that created a resilience/persistence and her generation helped pave the way for the rest of us. Mom, I salute you!

My dad gave me drive and ambition as well. From the earliest days of our lives, my dad told my sister and me that we could do anything we wanted to do. Starting in the third grade, he had me read the *Rocky Mountain News* and the *Denver Post* before he got home from work. I had to choose two articles to discuss before dinner. It was a great way to bond with him and to develop a nose for news. Now I do that every day with Bill Hemmer. But it started with my dad!

As my parents mentored me, so I have tried to pass on advice, tips, and strategies. No matter how much mentoring I do, the questions keep coming. Folks whom I mentored going into their first jobs are still asking me for advice as they take senior executive positions and juggle the work/life balance with multiple children and aging parents.

There's an insatiable demand for guidance, but a limited supply of the best answers. Add in the rapid advances in technology and artificial intelligence, and figuring out the post-Covid workplace, and we're all searching for answers to some pretty big questions.

So, I decided to put together something I think every reader will benefit from having on their nightstand.

A couple of years ago, I started a project for FoxNews .com called "Short Questions with Dana Perino." I often included questions asking my guests about the best advice they had ever received, and other questions about work, such as what did you want to be when you were growing up, what was your lucky break, and how did you manage to raise a family and succeed at your job?

The answers were amazing. For example, I knew Martha MacCallum wanted to be an actress—but I didn't know she also aspired to be an Olympic athlete (skiing). Trey Gowdy said he would have told his younger self to define success and significance according to your own terms—to be careful about the voices you allow into your life.

I spoke to dozens of colleagues and friends, authors, and experts for Short Questions. I loved their answers and wanted to share them more widely.

In this book, much like I do on my podcast, *Perino on Politics*, I reached out to my friends and trusted advisors to help me with the content. These are people I admire and to whom I've turned for advice over the years.

The book's chapters are based on the stages of career growth that I get questions about.

I've built the book like a ladder—as you move up at work, start a family, or find yourself managing a team, you can go back to those chapters and be reminded how you climbed those rungs and handled those challenges.

In each chapter you'll get advice and anecdotes and at the end I'll give you some suggestions for workplace etiquette in a post-Covid world, book and podcast recommendations, and some of my most tried-and-true advice.

So get ready. If you had trouble answering the question I started with, I hope that you'll find many pieces of advice here that you will use and pass on to others.

Because I wish someone had told me too.

Meet My Mentors

I am very excited to introduce you to the remarkable mentors featured in the pages ahead. Below you will find a brief bio of all my *I Wish Someone Had Told Me . . .* contributors. Each of these individuals holds a special place in my heart and has generously shared some of their best tried-and-true advice with you.

AINSLEY EARHARDT

Ainsley Earhardt brings the morning energy on Fox News. Ainsley has a journalism degree from the University of South Carolina. Her career began as a local news reporter in her home state of South Carolina before finding her home at Fox News Channel in 2007. In 2016 Ainsley became a prominent cohost of *Fox & Friends*, the top-rated morning program in cable news. She is enthusiastic, engaging, warm, professional, and funny. She brings an infectious energy to work and relies on her faith to reinforce her joy for life. Ainsley is also a best-selling author and I can attest that she's absolutely as nice in real life as she comes across on the screen.

ANDREA ARAGON

Andrea Aragon was my college roommate and my forever friend. She grew up in the small town of Rocky Ford, Colorado, with rural values and big-city dreams. She has had a lot of success and a ton of fun along the way. Currently Andrea is the executive director of the Robert Hoag Rawlings Foundation. She has over thirty years of experience in philanthropy and nonprofits. Prior to joining the foundation, she was the president/CEO of United Way of Pueblo County for seventeen years. She has received many awards for her community service and has served on several statewide and local boards. Andrea is currently a trustee of the El Pomar Foundation and Philanthropy Colorado. She and her husband, Darrin Smith, are the proud parents of two sons, Freddie and Evan.

BENJAMIN HALL

Benjamin Hall is one of the bravest men I've ever known. He is a fearless correspondent, reporting on the compelling stories happening around the world. His harrowing experience in Ukraine, where he survived a devastating attack that left him with severe injuries, is chronicled in his *New York Times* bestseller, *Saved: A War Reporter's Mission to Make It Home*. Despite facing unimaginable challenges, Benjamin's resilience shines through as he continues to cover major global events, including the Israel-Hamas conflict and the recent docuseries *Surviving Hamas*. While we first bonded over our love for dogs, we have since become close friends—he's brilliant, and a real gentleman—even if he is an Arsenal fan.

BILL HEMMER

What can I tell you about my co-anchor in work and life, **Bill Hemmer**? He's the same on- and off-screen—cheerful, joyous, funny, smart as heck, with a curious mind. He stands for me every time I take my seat at the anchor desk. He is a true family man and he's taught me so much about life, in addition to how to help break the news to our audience. He began his career in Cincinnati as a sports anchor, then took a major around-the-globe trip in his midtwenties, and since then has covered all of the big stories of our lives for the past three decades. I didn't know what my career was missing until I had a chance to work with him. What a pleasure it's been—and what great advice he provided for this book.

BRET BAIER

Bret Baier and I go way back, and my life has been better for it. We first met when I was a junior birdman at the White House and he was the Fox News correspondent. It is an honor to work and laugh with him. He's a joyous colleague. Bret currently anchors *Special Report with Bret Baier* on the Fox News Channel, and he and Martha anchor our election coverage and moderate the big debates. He joined FNC in 1998 as its first reporter in Atlanta. His accolades include the Horatio Alger Award for his commitment to education and charity, and recognition for *Special Report* as one of the most reliable news programs. He is also the author of several *New York Times* bestsellers. But Bret's favorite titles are husband and dad. And golfer!

BRIAN BRENBERG

Brian Brenberg is a wonderful Minnesota nice guy, with sharp financial insights and a commanding presence on Fox News and Fox Business. Brian cohosts *The Big Money*

Show on Fox Business alongside Jackie DeAngelis and Taylor Riggs, delivering expert analysis and commentary on the latest market trends. He is a teacher by instinct and experience, and I love learning from him. He's also a witty dad who shares his parenting life with humor and joy. Brian is a terrific colleague and friend.

BRIAN KILMEADE

There is no hour of the day that **Brian Kilmeade** isn't working and living his best life. Brian Kilmeade is a central figure at Fox News Channel, cohosting *Fox & Friends* and anchoring *One Nation with Brian Kilmeade* on Saturday night. He also hosts *The Brian Kilmeade Show*, a top-rated radio program with nearly two million podcast listeners. Brian knows a lot about a lot. He can talk sports, history, politics, foreign policy, and dogs. He's a terrific father, husband, and friend. I've never seen him in a bad mood, and I always love running into him in the hallways or on the sets. We all need some of his secret energy sauce, though even he isn't sure how he does it all.

CHARLES PAYNE

Charles Payne is one of my favorite people at Fox News Media. He brings energetic financial insights as the host of *Making Money with Charles Payne* and is a key voice in financial analysis. In 1991 Charles founded Wall Street Strategies, where he serves as CEO and principal analyst. Charles and I bonded over a long discussion about educational disparities for young people. He dedicates his time and resources to the Boys and Girls Club of Harlem, an organization that helped him get through some tough early days in his life. His books are impressive too. His latest is *Unstoppable Prosperity*, which is what he wants for everyone.

DAN BARR

Dan Barr is a new friend I met through one of my best mentors, Ed Gillespie. Ed and Dan went to college together and have remained good pals. So Dan and his wife, Paula, inherited me and my husband on a visit to Key West, Florida, in 2024. I had no idea I was going to end up with one of the best mentors for this book. Dan has an incredible history in human resources—he's worked at some of America's largest firms, as well as leading his own, Barr Resources. He is the proud father of four grown children and cares passionately about the people he helps place in America's great companies, as well as the young employees entering a rapidly changing world of work. He has keen insight into post-Covid workplaces, and his advice for those at the end of their careers is excellent.

DAVID BAHNSEN

David Bahnsen is a financial guru and a confident commentator on work, play, and life. When David talks, I listen. He is the founder, managing partner, and chief investment officer of the Bahnsen Group, a national private wealth management firm with offices across the country. David is consistently named one of the top financial advisors in America by *Barron's*, *Forbes*, and the *Financial Times*. He has written several bestselling books and is frequently a guest on CNBC,

Bloomberg, and Fox Business. His most recent book, *Full-Time: Work and the Meaning of Life,* is a must-read.

DIERKS BENTLEY

The first time I met **Dierks Bentley**, a friend asked me, "Was he so glad to meet you?" And I had to admit, "He had no idea who I was." He has had multiple consecutive hits, including three on his album *Home* and three on his album *Riser.* Fast-forward and over the years we have become friends, and I'm honored to know him. I had emerged from the White House without an iPod and almost a decade of listening only to news on the radio. Soon after, on the train back and forth from Washington, D.C., to New York, I became a superfan. I admire Dierks for many reasons: he's stayed true to his roots; he loves his family and has built a wonderful life for them while he protects their privacy; he leads a band that puts on the very best show every night of their tours; and he's worked so hard, never taking any shortcuts. And he's chosen to remain humble and faithful. They don't make them better than Dierks. (Hey, put that line in a song!)

DR. MARK SHRIME

Mark G. Shrime, MD, MPH, PhD, FACS (yes, he's earned *all* of the letters), is an internationally recognized surgeon and currently serves as the International Chief Medical Officer at Mercy Ships and a lecturer in Global Health and Social Medicine at Harvard Medical School. I met him on a visit to Mercy Ships in Congo just after he'd saved a little boy's life with a miraculously timed surgery. We became fast friends—and he answered all of my questions, even the dumb ones. I encouraged him to write his excellent book, *Solving for Why*, which reflects his journey to find deeper meaning and fulfillment. Outside of his professional life, Dr. Shrime is an avid photographer, public speaker, and rock climber, having competed on *American Ninja Warrior* in multiple seasons.

ELISE BITTER

One of the surprising things in life is realizing you have so much to learn from people younger than you. **Elise Bitter** is that person for me. I met her through mutual friends at the Jersey Shore. She's a licensed psychotherapist and clinical supervisor at her New York City–based private practice, which specializes in counseling high achievers. Elise's areas of expertise include anxiety reduction, relationship issues (romantic, family, peer), life transitions, and executive coaching. I have enjoyed getting to know her on walks and on the tennis court. She helps me understand what younger people are going through. She's wise beyond her years and now the mother to two boys who keep her on her toes. She manages all of her roles with grace and grit, alongside her retired Navy SEAL husband, Matt.

FRANCINE LEFRAK

Francine LeFrak is the president of the Francine A. LeFrak Foundation and the Same Sky Foundation. You may be familiar with her from the times I've spotlighted her foundation as my "One More Thing" on *The Five*. Francine is one of the brightest points of light I have ever known. She has the wherewithal to do anything she wants any time she wants. And what she chooses and wants to do is help others, especially those in Africa. She has blown me away with her vision, her kindness, and most notably, her results. She believes there's abundant talent, but not enough opportunities. So she's made it her mission to fix that. Francine is a wonderful friend too—she is thoughtful and generous with her most valuable asset: her time.

FRANK SILLER

Frank Siller is chairman and CEO of the Tunnel to Towers Foundation, which honors his brother Stephen Siller, a New York City firefighter who perished on 9/11, by leading a foundation dedicated to preserving his legacy of heroism. On September 11, Stephen, after completing a night shift with FDNY's Squad 1, turned back to help when he heard of the attacks, running through the Brooklyn Battery Tunnel to reach the South Tower of the World Trade Center. Grieving his loss, Frank founded the Tunnel to Towers Foundation to commemorate Stephen's sacrifice. Through its mission, the foundation continues to honor and support America's heroes and their families. I have loved getting to know Frank—his approach to life is one to emulate.

GREG GUTFELD

I joke that **Greg Gutfeld** is the brother I never wanted, though the truth is he's the best colleague I could have ever asked for when I joined Fox News Channel. We didn't know each other well until we were seated next to each other on a temporary and experimental show called *The Five* in 2011. They put us together because we were the shortest and our pairing worked best for lighting. And, it turns out, for ratings. Greg brought me out of my shell and pushed me to be myself on camera. I will always be grateful for that. Sometimes we wonder how it is that we were never fired—though they've kept us on and expanded our roles. We are each other's longest-serving workmates, and I'm thrilled for his success and enjoy the wit and wisdom he brings to the shows. I also love his writing. He's a disciplined thinker and writer and always hits home runs with his books. And I finally prevailed on one aspect of his life. In 2022, Greg became the owner of Gus, the cutest French bulldog I've ever seen. So I guess I can say, I win!

HAROLD FORD JR.

Harold Ford Jr. is America's favorite political analyst, and for good reason. He's the most thoughtful person on-air, and he makes excellent points without rubbing people the wrong way. I knew Harold from afar when I was in the White House and he was a congressman from his beloved home state of Tennessee. Little did we know that one day we would work together on America's most popular cable program. I've enjoyed learning from his broad and deep base of knowledge, but what's really impressed me over the years is his dedication to his wife and children, as well as the fact he has friends from his early childhood that he still talks to every day. Harold is a man who shows up for everyone. If we could clone him, we would. But Harold Ford Jr. is one of a kind, and aren't we fortunate to have him in our lives.

JACKIE DEANGELIS

Jackie DeAngelis brings her financial expertise and vibrant energy to Fox Business Network, where she has been a key financial correspondent since April 2019. She's the cohost of *The Big Money Show* with Taylor Riggs and Brian Brenberg, offering clever market insights and engaging commentary. When Jackie went through a major health concern, she did so with such strength and dignity that she inspired me to keep her approach to life in mind no matter what challenge it put in front of me. She is thoughtful, gracious, and confident—a perfect blend of an analyst and a storyteller.

JESSE WATTERS

When **Jesse Watters** joined *The Five*, I didn't know that he would become not only a close friend but also like my kid brother who kept getting into trouble while making me laugh the entire time. I love when I have to hold his hand when he's about to say something inappropriate—he skirts that fine line better than anyone I know. I so enjoy his commentary and his books, and I appreciate our collaboration on emails and texts that probably drive him crazy but he's too polite to tell me to stop. He's the star of *Jesse Watters Primetime*, and I am glad to be included in his world, along with his wife, Emma, who loves to share books with me. Jesse's most important job is being a dad, and his four children sure are fortunate to have him as the head of their household. I look forward to seeing all that comes next for him. I'll be there to hold his hand, while blushing and cringing, any time he wants.

JESSICA TARLOV

Jessica Tarlov is a wise young woman who has been a part of Fox News Channel since 2017. She is part of our little show, *The Five*, as one of the cohosts. She has strong beliefs and explains them well, cheerfully sparring with the team on every show. She also is a dedicated family woman, with a wonderful love story of meeting her husband in an elevator in New York City. She is a mom of two daughters, and she didn't even hold it against me when I accidentally spilled the beans that she was pregnant on the show. (In my defense, she was seven and a half months along!) Jessica is also vice president of research and consumer insight for Bustle Digital Group. And she's a wiz at all things entertainment. She curates recommendations for each of us on the show—knowing what we would like, and she loves professional basketball. She's a catch all around.

JIMMY FAILLA

Jimmy Failla is a former New York City cabdriver turned comedian. He's become a prominent voice at Fox News since joining as a writer in 2016 and one of our dearest friends. He and his wife, Jenny, and their son, Lincoln, fit right into our family. His humor sometimes makes me yell, "JIMMY!" in all caps, to which he just lands another joke that makes me laugh and cringe. Jimmy hosts *Fox News Saturday Night* and the *Fox Across America* radio show. His radio program started with the beginning of Covid in March 2020 on twenty-seven stations, and it now airs on over 150 stations nationwide. Jimmy also authored *Cancel Culture Dictionary*, showcasing his witty takes on current events. He's a funny guy and a wise guy. But not a wiseguy. Listen, learn, and laugh with Jimmy. It's one of my favorite things to do.

JOHN ROBERTS

John Roberts and I have a friendship that goes way back to my White House days. When I first met him, I was working as the deputy press secretary and he was a correspondent for CBS. Fast-forward and today he co-anchors *America Reports with John Roberts & Sandra Smith* on Fox News Channel, bringing his extensive reporting experience to the forefront. Since joining FNC in 2011, Roberts has covered a range of high-profile stories, from the Israel-Hamas conflict to exclusive interviews with key members of the Biden administration. Known for his excellent interviewing skills and breaking-news coverage, he's navigated the complexities of the Trump administration as FNC's chief White House correspondent, reported live from international summits, and tackled major events like the 2016 presidential election and the Ebola outbreak. A Canadian by birth, Roberts previously anchored CNN's *American Morning* and prior to that spent fourteen years with CBS News. He is a wonderful husband and father to twin teenagers, for which he also deserves a medal for Dad of the Year!

JOHNNY JOEY JONES

Johnny Joey Jones is our go-to guy for military analysis across all Fox News Media platforms. Joey's not just a TV personality; he's also a *New York Times* bestselling author with his book *Unbroken Bonds of Battle*, which honors the brave service members who protect our freedoms. Before his media career, Joey served in the United States Marine Corps, completing two combat deployments. He was inspired to enlist after terrorists attacked our nation on September 11, 2001. However, his journey took a dramatic turn in 2010 when an IED-related incident in Afghanistan resulted in the loss of both legs above the knee and serious injuries to his arms. Joey didn't let that stop him. He has channeled his experience into advocacy, working tirelessly to improve the lives of veterans and their families. I lean on him for wise counsel on the many challenges facing our military and veterans, as well as to better understand sports. He's one of my secret weapons for sounding like I know a little about what I'm saying.

JEANINE PIRRO

Judge Jeanine Pirro is one of my cohosts on *The Five*, where she brings her sharp wit, stylish outfits, and legal expertise to the table every weekday. Since joining Fox in 2006, Jeanine has been a powerhouse, first as a legal analyst and then as the host of the must-watch *Justice with Judge Jeanine*, for eleven years. But her impressive career began long before her TV stardom. As the first woman elected Westchester County, New York, district attorney, Jeanine made history by tackling tough cases and launching the first domestic violence unit in a prosecutor's office nationwide. She also shattered glass ceilings as the first female Westchester County Court judge and later chaired the New York State Commission on Domestic Violence Fatality Review Board. She is a proud mother and grandmother, and she has four dogs that keep her on her toes. We are all looking for her secret to strong energy—she could bottle that up and sell it for millions.

LAUREN FRITTS

Lauren Fritts has been one of my very best friends since I joined Fox News Channel in 2009. We met at Fox News on an assignment for Sean Hannity and a deep friendship was born over the worst gas station food we could find for our week on the road. But aside from our friendship, Lauren has nearly two decades of experience leading public affairs, communications, brand, and marketing teams. Most recently, she served as chief corporate affairs and marketing officer at WeWork, playing a critical role in the company's turnaround. Before WeWork, Lauren was digital director and deputy communications director for New Jersey governor Chris Christie and spent nearly a decade as a producer at Fox News Channel. She has incredible instincts for excellent communication and has become the leader and manager that all of us want to be. Lauren is also a very talented artist and has a sweet dog named Charlie, so I'm keeping her around forever.

LAWRENCE JONES

Lawrence Jones is the tallest younger brother I could have ever hoped for. We were immediate friends when he burst onto the scene at Fox News Media in 2018, quickly making his mark with compelling storytelling and relatable "man-on-the-street" segments that spotlight local community issues. He's now one of the cohosts of *Fox & Friends* on weekdays. When he first came to Fox, I chided him for being from Texas but not liking or even understanding country music. He's come a long way on that front. Lawrence is a crowd favorite across the country, and while I'm happy to share him with everyone, my favorite moments are the private mentoring lunches we have together. I learn as much from him as he does from me. And my late dog Jasper was the first dog he ever loved. Now Lawrence helps veterans and active military by promoting the importance of our K9 companions. He's raising Nala to help raise awareness—and now they're the best pair around.

LYDIA HU

Lydia Hu is one of my mentees at Fox News and it's been a joy to watch her grow. She joined Fox Business Network in 2021, not long after making a career transition from law to journalism. From agriculture to energy, real estate to travel, she covers it all with an eye for detail and a passion for storytelling. She jumped right in to help me write some questions about parenting and childcare before the GOP debate in 2023. With multiple New York Emmy Awards under her belt, she is a trusted voice in business news, blending her rich background in law and journalism to shine a light on the issues that matter most. Her role as a mother of two always provides me with additional insight that I value beyond measure.

MARTHA MACCALLUM

Martha MacCallum's career journey is as varied as it is impressive. I am in awe of her skills, talents, wisdom, and wit. Martha began her journey by earning her political science degree at St. Lawrence University and then kicked off her media career as a freelance researcher for *Corporate Finance* magazine. Her path led her through various roles at NBC from 1997 to 2003 and before joining Fox News in 2004, she made her mark as an anchor and reporter at WBIS-TV and as a business correspondent at Wall Street Journal Television. Since joining Fox, Martha has anchored *The Story with Martha MacCallum*, cohosted major election coverage, and hosted the podcast *The Untold Story with Martha MacCallum*. She coleads our election night coverage and debate moderation. She's one of the funniest people I've had the pleasure to work with. If you only knew the looks we give each other during big speeches and debates we are covering. I also love her book, *Unknown Valor*, and was honored to be one of the early readers of that bestseller. She's a wonderful wife and mom of three thriving young adults. She also loves dogs!

MICHELE CHASE

Michele Chase is one of the coolest people I've ever known. She is a Chief People Officer with twenty-plus years of experience across public relations, financial communications, and in sports, cable, and music. Michele is a trusted strategic business partner and advisor to CEOs and senior leadership. She is skilled in leading organizations through restructurings and mergers, creating HR infrastructure, handling conflict resolution, and managing the most complex employee relations issues and actions. She's unflappable and dignified, and is known for being gracious under pressure, with an emphasis on transparency, and for being an HR "go to" person across markets, staff levels, and regions. In addition to being the

People Lead, her favorite role is being the mom of three boys and two dogs. She also has good friends dating back to her childhood—the mark of a great person.

MIKE ROWE

Mike Rowe is a man of many hats: Emmy-winning TV host, producer, narrator, podcaster, and bestselling author. Best known for *Dirty Jobs*, where he dives into America's dirtiest professions, he's become a champion for the skilled trades. Through his mikeroweWORKS Foundation, he has awarded nearly $7 million in scholarships and pushed for shop class revival. He has narrated everything from *Deadliest Catch* to wildebeest meals on National Geographic, and his podcast, *The Way I Heard It*, has been downloaded nearly 300 million times. Always up for a challenge, Mike's latest venture includes a delicious Tennessee whiskey named Knobel. Though he's wary of TikTok, he keeps fans engaged on Facebook and occasionally YouTube. He's the best storyteller I've ever seen. What an honor it is to call him a friend.

MORA NEILSON

Mora Neilson and I met because of a joint love—mentoring and fashion. She asked me what she should wear to the White House Correspondents Association Dinner and we've been close friends ever since. Mora is the cofounder of Neilson Swiader, an integrated marketing communications agency. I remember when she worried about becoming an entrepreneur. I told her to go for it. And she's crushing it, which is no surprise. Mora is an award-winning global communications leader with more than twenty years of experience in consumer engagement strategies and execution within beauty, fashion, and entertainment. Prior to starting her business, Mora spent more than a decade leading integrated marketing communications for L'Oréal Paris, the number one beauty company in the world.

NORBERT FRASSA

Norbert Frassa has been a friend of ours for over twenty-five years—he also has helped us save and invest during our marriage. Norbert works for Morgan Stanley; his title there is financial advisor. While he's well qualified, holding both Certified Financial Planner and Certified Portfolio Manager designations, he is also very down-to-earth and knows how to calm people (okay, me) down and to help them realize that, yes, everything will be okay. Norbert is passionate and dedicated to making sure his clients have confidence and power through knowledge, and he believes in the transformational power of financial education. He also has an amazing lemon tree and sends me some of his best every season. Now *that's* how to keep a customer happy!

PATTI CALLAHAN HENRY

Patti Callahan Henry and I were friends before I ever knew she was an author and a novelist. So, finding that out was the cherry on top of the sundae for me. Patti is a *New York Times*, *Globe and Mail*, and *USA Today* bestselling author of seventeen novels, including her newest, *The Secret Book of Flora Lea*. She's also a podcast host of original content for her novels *Surviving Savannah* and *Becoming Mrs. Lewis*. We first bonded in South Carolina, with our dogs, her husband, and their three children. I love her story of becoming a writer and appreciate her never-ending list of good recommendations for me to read, as well as her encouragement of me to write a work of fiction. Thank you, Patti—you never know, I just might do it!

PAUL MAURO

Paul Mauro is a contributor for Fox News Media providing legal and criminal justice analysis. Currently Mauro works as an attorney at DeMarco Law. Previously he served as the commanding officer of the New York City Police Department's Legal Bureau and the Executive Officer of the Intelligence Operations and Analysis Bureau. He earned his master's of public administration from Harvard University's Kennedy School of Government and received his JD from Fordham Law School. Paul has written for the *Wall Street Journal*, *New York Post*, *Washington Times*, and other publications. He's also one of the best editors for all of us writing books—including this one. What a gift his friendship is.

PETER MCMAHON

Peter McMahon and I met on a plane in 1997. It was love at first flight. We married in 1998. He's been my most trusted and valued companion and mentor as well as the best husband I could have ever been blessed to have. He is British by birth and American by choice. Peter has had an extensive career in medical device sales. He is renowned for his outstanding innovative and leadership qualities in this business. With friends all over the world from his career, Peter currently serves as president of GreenSleeve Surgical, a company he founded earlier this year. He's also our dog, Percy's, very favorite human. Mine too!

PHIL LAGO

Phil Lago is one of the best mentors I've ever had. He guided me through so many complex foreign policy issues during my time as the White House press secretary. Phil spent thirty years in government and held prominent positions at the U.S. Central Intelligence Agency, National Geospatial-Intelligence Agency, and National Security Council at the White House. After leaving government, he served as executive director of Blackbird Technologies and then cofounded the Command Consulting Group in Washington D.C. He also advised heads of state and senior government leaders across South and Central America, the Middle East, and Africa. Phil is committed to philanthropy and has officiated high school basketball and football, and coached both boys' and girls' athletics teams. He also mentored high school students through the Take Stock in Children of Florida program, and now enjoys retirement, relishing outdoor activities with his wife.

I'll never forget when I brought my niece to work one day—she thought she wanted to grow up to be a spy—and Phil took her everywhere and arranged for her to meet with several women in the CIA so she could hear about their experiences. Phil has always gone over and beyond, and I'm grateful to have him in my life.

SALENA ZITO

Salena Zito knows America and she is a great person to know. Her career followed an excellent trail of grit, hard work, and taking her mentors' advice. Today Salena is a western Pennsylvania–based national reporter for the *Washington Examiner*, contributor to the *Wall Street Journal* and the *Free Press*, and coauthor of *The Great Revolt: Inside the Populist Coalition Reshaping American Politics*. Salena approaches reporting from the back roads of the country listening to the views of Americans who are often overlooked by our national media as the coverage by local news organizations shrinks. Most importantly, she is a mother and grandmother. And let me tell you—this woman can also cook up a storm. Can't wait to share a meal with her one day.

SANDRA SMITH

My friend **Sandra Smith** is the co-anchor of *America Reports* on Fox News Channel, where she brings clarity to the day's biggest headlines with a dash of southern charm. Since joining Fox in 2007, Sandra has played a prominent role on the channel. With a background in finance and a stint at Bloomberg TV, she's no stranger to high-stakes reporting. Before coming to Fox, Sandra was an on-air reporter for Bloomberg Television, where she covered U.S. equities and derivatives markets. In addition to her work, Sandra is raising two children, dominates the tennis court, and takes care of her beloved dog. She's also an avid sailor and knows just when to pick all the blueberries. Sandra is a woman of many talents indeed, and I'm honored to know her.

STEVE DOOCY

Steve Doocy is a generous colleague to everyone he works with. I remember how he stayed late one day to help me learn how to read a teleprompter—patiently answering all of my questions. Steve is a cornerstone of Fox News Channel as the cohost of *Fox & Friends*, where he has been delivering the latest news and engaging interviews since 1998. Rising through the ranks from a weather reporter to one of the most recognizable faces in morning television, Doocy has helped *Fox & Friends* maintain its position as the top-rated cable news morning show for over two decades. I also appreciate how he's never lost his Kansas outlook. We share that down-on-the-farm feeling and I so enjoy our chats whenever we get together. It has been fun to watch his three children grow into these talented young people who are now making Steve and Kathy the happiest of grandparents.

STUART VARNEY

Stuart Varney and I go way back to the days when I first joined Fox News in 2009. We were paired on Sean Hannity's show once a week for five years. I looked forward to those Tuesday nights because we always had a laugh and I learned something new. I also loved to make fun of his "posh" accent, and he'd say, "It is *not* posh!" We bonded over those years and I am honored to have his wisdom in this book. Born in the United Kingdom, Varney has traveled the globe. After secondary school, he spent a year working in Nairobi, Kenya, before returning home and graduating from the London School of Economics. Prior to joining FNC, Varney served as the host of CNBC's *Wall Street Journal Editorial Board with Stuart Varney*. I had the pleasure of co-moderating the second Republican presidential primary debate in September 2023 with him. And while sometimes it didn't feel like we would, we lived to tell the tale.

TAYLOR RIGGS

Taylor Riggs is a wonderfully talented young woman. She joined Fox Business Network in December 2022, bringing a wealth of experience to her role as cohost of *The Big Money Show* alongside Jackie DeAngelis and Brian Brenberg. Her career, which began in municipal bond reporting, includes nine years at Bloomberg News, where she co-anchored a daily program and spearheaded coverage of equities, bonds, currencies, and commodities. Riggs, a graduate of New York University with a degree in journalism and communication studies, holds a master's in finance from Johns Hopkins University's Carey Business School and is currently pursuing a juris doctor at New York Law School. She has also achieved Chartered Financial Analyst (CFA) certification at all three levels, reflecting her deep expertise in finance. While doing all of that, she also got her most cherished title—that of mother. Watch this girl—her star is sure to keep rising.

TOM SHILLUE

Tom Shillue has been a lively voice on Fox News since 2015, where he serves as a contributor and regularly appears as a panelist on *Gutfeld!* (weeknights at 11 p.m. eastern). Before his role on *Gutfeld!*, Shillue was known for his work as the xxxvi | Meet My Mentors

host of *Red Eye*, where he led a spirited roundtable discussion on the day's top stories. A seasoned stand-up comedian, Shillue also made his mark as a correspondent on Comedy Central's *The Daily Show with Jon Stewart* and has showcased his comedic talent on NBC's *The Tonight Show*. His storytelling prowess earned him accolades from the ECNY, winning Best Storyteller in 2011 and Best One Person Show in 2010. I love his approach to life, and his book, *Mean Dads*, is a fantastic memoir and parenting handbook all in one. You can't help but smile when Tom enters a room. What a talent he is.

TREY GOWDY

Harold Watson "Trey" Gowdy III has worn many hats throughout his career: federal prosecutor, solicitor for South Carolina's Seventh Judicial Circuit, four-term U.S. representative, and chair of the House Oversight Committee. He hosts the weekly show *Sunday Night in America with Trey Gowdy* on Fox News. Trey utilizes his legal and sharp practical analysis to help us understand today's pressing issues. He has such a way with words (and the thoughts and ideas behind them). He always has a genuine compliment waiting for everyone he meets and checks in on his friends on good and bad days. I highly recommend his book *Start, Stay, or Leave—The Art of Decision Making* to everyone. It was one of the best self-help books I've ever read in my life (and I've read a lot of them!).

TYRUS

George Murdoch, best known for his wrestling nickname **Tyrus**, is my biggest friend—and one of my closest. He is a

Fox News contributor and a regular guest on *The Greg Gutfeld Show*. A former college football player, professional wrestler, actor, and entertainer, Tyrus combines his wit and humor in his commentary across various Fox News programs, in his bestselling books, and onstage at his live shows. Hailing from Los Angeles, Tyrus's early life was marked by instability, bouncing around foster homes at an early age. As he got older, his formidable frame (standing at six feet eight!) led to jobs in security, which subsequently resulted in him joining hip-hop superstar Snoop Dogg's security team. In 2006 Tyrus made his pro wrestling debut with WWE. By 2014 he had adopted the ring name Tyrus for Total Impact Wrestling. Aside from his stage presence, his favorite role is dad to his children and caretaker of his many pets. We're an odd couple, and I love it.

I Wish Someone
Had Told Me . . .

CHAPTER 1

Lift Off!

(Deciding What to Do)

I wanted to be an Olympic gymnast. Cathy Rigby was the first one I ever admired. She was powerful, skilled, graceful, and a winner. A courageous competitor. Plus, I kind of looked like her. Or wanted to—she was short like me!

I could do cartwheels on the balance beam. I could tumble across the backyard of our house on Elm Street in Denver, Colorado. I could spring fast to the vault and stick the landing on the mat. And I could dream.

In third grade, I remember the librarian at Ellis Elementary School handing me a book, *Cathy Rigby: On the Beam*. I read that book several times and memorized it. I can still picture the photographs in my mind.

A great book from an even better librarian. My worlds collided. Gymnastics . . . in a book. Could anything be more perfect for me?

In 1984, I cheered on Mary Lou Retton to her perfect 10 at those Olympic games. America the beautiful, *indeed*! The

United States was the *best* and *Reagan* was our *president* and we were on top of the *world*.

It was my "you go girl" moment of the 1980s.

The following year, during a practice at the YMCA on Colorado Boulevard, I realized something: I was never going to the Olympics (unless I bought a ticket). I couldn't do the double backflips and full twists that my teammates mastered. I wasn't there and I was going to have to let that dream go. I could feel that sting of disappointment in myself, with some embarrassment thrown in. I didn't have the talent of some of my peers. I continued to be on the school team for another year but then I gave it up.

Instead of gymnastics, I joined the speech team. And the rest is history.

Well . . . history in the making, as this book will spell out.

With every child, there are the hopes and dreams of his or her parents regarding what they'll do, how they'll live, and whether they'll be happy.

Now some people know exactly what they want to do for a career when they grow up. It's a question you hear often: What do you want to be when you grow up? We expect to hear answers like football player, doctor, pilot, Navy SEAL, teacher, singer . . . and now, YouTube influencer.

But it's very common that what someone wants to do when they're a kid is not what they end up doing for work as an adult.

So why do we keep pestering kids with this question? I suppose it's because we want them to think ahead, to have dreams—and a belief that maybe we can help them achieve their goals.

The social psychologist, Adam Grant, wrote in his book

Originals that we should stop asking kids that. It stunts their creative thinking and puts them in a box. I get his point, yet I still find myself asking the question. I ask Greg Gutfeld almost daily.

As a mentor, I love to give counsel to people of all ages—especially young teens. I admire their optimism and enthusiasm for ideas. I like to help channel them in the right direction. And I love to give them reading assignments.

I realize that for many, especially with the world of work changing so much since Covid and with all the new technologies disrupting entire industries, that deciding what you want to do, what you want to study, and where you want to live are really challenging questions.

What does a career in the second quarter of the twenty-first century look like? I am not sure of the answer to that. But I know who to ask.

The following is a compilation of the best answers I received to this basic question of what do you want to do and when did you know. I posed this to a variety of people I admire, both those who always knew what they wanted to do, and those who had no clue and ended up in the careers they have now.

That's the more likely scenario, by the way—sometimes you just start working and figure it out. Maybe the best answer is this: you don't need to know right now.

In 2023, I attended a birthday party for my friend's one-year-old son. In keeping with the Korean tradition of Dol-janchi to celebrate the milestone birthday, he and his proud mother were traditionally dressed in colorful silks.

There were many delicious Korean snacks, including rice cakes and special fruits. After a ceremonial prayer it was time for the fortune-telling. This young boy was going to show his family and friends what he would be when he grew up.

Several toys representing different professions were laid out on the table: a judge's gavel, a pencil, a ruler, a stethoscope, a handheld microphone, etc. He looked at all of them. He took his time. We held our breath. What was it going to be?

He reached out his hand, hovered over the gavel (oh! we have a future lawyer!) but no, he wanted something different. Alas, he moved on and picked up. . . . the microphone.

So, look out, BTS—we have a performer on the way!

It's a lovely and fun tradition that helps predict a child's future. I think of it often.

If we aren't certain what we want to do, or we are being discouraged because it isn't practical, maybe we can reach down and choose something else.

Besides, we're in America, where choices can freely be made. Take advantage of that—no matter what stage of your career you're in. There's a bright future ahead for all of us.

Whether you realize it or not, the choices are there on the table in front of you. Here are the experiences of some people I trust—to guide your hand.

MARTHA MACCALLUM

Many of us have big dreams when we are young. You once told me that you wanted to be a Broadway star and an Olympian when you grew up. How did that vision evolve throughout your lifetime? When did you decide what to major in at college? Would you have ever imagined you'd end up where you are today?

Ha. Well, obviously neither one of those worked out! I just always knew I wanted to do something big and interesting. In college I embraced political science and theater—back and forth between law school and the stage. The stage won and I was off to a two-year postgraduate program at Circle in the Square Theater in New York. It was a magical time for me, waitressing to pay the rent and taking classes all day—Shakespeare, scene study, voice, movement, and even stage-fighting with swords.

But then as life would have it, although I was auditioning and doing some bit parts and off-off (!) Broadway plays, part-time work at a financial magazine doing editorial work led to a job offer. I was anxious to take it on, and the articles I wrote there allowed me to build a portfolio of bylines, and got me a job as a producer at Wall Street Journal Television. There I produced segments and eventually began some work in front of the camera, then it was on to CNBC, and then I got a call from Fox, and that really changed my life.

I made the leap and it has been such an amazing journey full of incredible experiences from elections, to travel around the world, from London for royal family coverage to Iwo Jima to writing *Unknown Valor*. I'm grateful for the team I work with at Fox and the extraordinary people I've been privileged to meet and interview. And no, I never imagined I would end up here, but if you keep following your dream, wherever it leads, the surprises are the best part.

DIERKS BENTLEY

Reflecting on your journey, can you pinpoint the moment in your life when you decided you wanted to pursue country music as a career? What advice would you offer to someone who feels pressured to pursue a career path dictated more by societal expectations than by their true interests?

I feel very fortunate that I had a moment when I was seventeen when I knew exactly what I wanted to do with my life. A friend of mine played me a Hank Williams Jr. song and I just remember thinking, "This is it. This is what I've been searching for." And I'm lucky that that dream I was chasing was really more of an obsession. I felt like I had no choice but to do everything I could to put myself in a position to find success.

That said, there were certainly a lot of times of self-doubt and financial concern. I remember at one point just being tired of having to call home for money and thinking I should put my college degree to use. I went and interviewed with a money management firm that I had previously interned with. And I remember feeling pretty defeated about it all. I called my mom and she said, "You need to follow your bliss," a quote I later learned was associated with Joseph Campbell. I would pass that same advice along to any younger folks out there. Do what you love to do, and let success come find you.

TREY GOWDY

It's quite remarkable how life can come full circle—from your days as a newspaper delivery boy in Spartanburg, South Carolina, to now delivering national news on Sunday Night in America *on* Fox. *Reflecting on your first job, are there any standout experiences that have left a lasting impact on you? And if so, how did that experience shape your approach to work today?*

A couple of things stand out: I learned I was not a morning person! Four a.m. came brutally for a kid in high school. I learned to deal with fear. It was dark. It was cold. I was on a *moped* miles from home at an hour when most folks are asleep. I learned not to let the episodic take over the normal. I would always glance at the paper before I began rolling them and putting a rubber band around them or placing them in plastic bags if it was raining. Stories about a random kidnapping or a violent crime in some faraway state always caught my attention and made me more fearful.

What we put into our heads usually dictates how we view the world. I had to persuade myself that just because something bad happened in Kansas or Ohio did not mean something bad was going to happen to me that morning in Spartanburg, South Carolina.

I also had to deliver a newspaper to an office in a mortuary in the middle of a cemetery. That was quite the experience every morning in the dark, driving past headstones and markers wondering who they were one hundred years ago and who would drive past my own grave site one hundred years from now.

Lastly, I learned the least expected from people are the nicest ones and the ones you think would be nice often aren't. One of my own church members was the first to call and complain when the paper was a minute late. People I never actually met included a Christmas bonus with the December payment.

BILL HEMMER

In "Short Questions with Dana Perino," you defined success as "doing something you love to do." How has your measurement of success changed and evolved throughout your lifetime?

Between the ages of sixteen and twenty-one, I bopped around nineteen different jobs. I swept floors at my high school, I washed dishes, I bused tables at restaurants, I worked in the produce department for a grocery store, I worked in a nursery taking care of massive trees, I drove a Ford stake-body truck through Ohio, Indiana, and Kentucky delivering rebuilt motors. So I did a lot. But one thing that struck me early in television: if you're going to do something for thirty years, you better find a job that challenges your brain. If you keep your mind engaged, you'll never get bored. I found that job.

LYDIA HU

After practicing law in Baltimore for five years, you made the transition to journalism. What's one skill you learned as an attorney that you find yourself using each day in your current role?

I cannot think of a better way to have started my professional life than being a lawyer. Among the many lessons I carry with me today, I learned it's important to consider other perspectives. One need not agree, but listening is crucial.

I was a commercial litigation associate, which is a fancy way to say I was a civil trial lawyer usually representing businesses and employers. By the time the case would reach my desk, parties had probably tried unsuccessfully to resolve their costly disagreement.

Listening to one's own client is obviously critical.

Considering the opposing party's views is equally important, and sometimes very difficult. Tensions could be high, patience with the opposing party short.

But I learned the simple act of listening intently offered benefits, even when agreement is elusive. Oftentimes, insight is gained that affirms one's own view or perhaps offers a fresh perspective. Relationships are forged. Respect is conveyed.

BRET BAIER

You've said the key thing for you in big interviews is listening. Being able to listen to the person you are interviewing and re-acting in real time. In Everything Will Be Okay, *I wrote that being a good listener is key to becoming a good leader. If you can demonstrate the qualities of someone who should be listened to and followed, you'll earn the title of "leader." Could you speak to this and share any strategies you have found most effective in cultivating active listening skills?*

Listen first is what I say. It makes you better in all aspects. Ask more questions than you make statements and be interested—and interesting. Overall, most people like to hear themselves talk. If you can listen and hear them, they are more likely to listen to you when it's important to you.

TREY GOWDY

What advice would you give to someone who feels pressured to choose a career path but is still exploring their interests and passions?

Decide what kind of person you are. Are you someone whose work dictates your self-image, your self-value, the way you see yourself? Do you determine any aspect of your self-worth from what you do as opposed to who you are?

If what you do professionally or workwise impacts how you view yourself, you need to acknowledge that or change how you view yourself. Some view work as simply a means of provision that enables them to pursue other things that mean more—like hobbies, or travel, or time with family. It is truly and simply a means to an end, but you must recognize that and know who you are for that season of life to make things go smoothly for you.

That season of life will change and so too may your view of yourself and what is important. A recurring theme for me is to define significance for yourself and to pursue significance over success. Success is often defined by others: money, fame, titles, accolades, etc.

Define a significant life for yourself and then pursue that even if the trappings of what others call "success" never come.

JOHN ROBERTS

What advice would you give to someone who feels pressured to choose a career path but is still exploring their interests and passions?

You will never be happy unless you are doing what you love. I wake up every day looking forward to what the day holds. Life is long. There are plenty of roads you can go down in exploring your passions. Like me, many people end up doing something completely different than they first envisioned.

And don't let anyone tell you that you can't achieve what you are passionate about. When I made the jump from music television to news, I was ridiculed. But I never got dismayed. I simply kept my eye on the task in front of me, and worked at it as hard as I could. Throughout my career, Winston Churchill's words rang in my head: "Never, ever, ever, ever, ever give up."

PHIL LAGO

What factors did you consider when choosing your career path and how did you know it was the right fit for you? How do you think one can identify their passions and align them with a fulfilling career?

Embrace the saying, "Be yourself, as everyone else is already taken." Leaders cannot be copied; the six leaders I admire most have unique operating styles that made them stand out. They lead in different ways, based on the situation, their personalities, experiences, instincts, and luck. Certainly you can and should try to emulate some of their behaviors, but understand leaders who had great success also had many failures. History is filled with leaders such as Ulysses S. Grant, who was a great general but, at best, a mediocre president. Other leaders either stayed too long or failed to evolve with the times. Being a good leader involves paying attention, listening, and learning.

Warren Buffett once opined that the key to making friends and getting along with coworkers is learning to change your behavior as you mature. You do this by emulating those you admire and adopting the qualities they possess. Before you become a good leader you have to become a good team member.

Unleash your inner leader. This requires self-awareness of your personal strengths and weaknesses. You should also adopt positive qualities like integrity and empathy, combined with genuine, transparent interactions. Seek feedback and criticism from diverse perspectives; foster a collaborative environment that promotes open communication, creativity, and calculated risk-taking. Recognize that your organization's most valued asset should be its intellectual capital, and that each individual has unique strengths and weaknesses. Create an inclusive environment where everyone can work together effectively. It is your responsibility to get everyone to work together. Don't mess this up. Encourage and incentivize this behavior.

BRIAN KILMEADE

Could you elaborate on the decision-making process that led you to start a career in broadcasting and radio?

I always loved the idea of broadcasting to people I can't see but know are there. I loved it from the first time I used a CB radio. I love TV, but I love the freedom of radio even more. Most of all, I love live entertainment. I sense anything can happen, and I can respond instinctively.

MIKE ROWE

What role do you believe education plays in shaping a person's life?

It's certainly true that degrees and diplomas and certifications shape the way other people perceive us, and those perceptions will likely determine quite a bit about who we become. But in reality, an education is not nearly as valuable as a curious mind. Curious people are more likely to assume risk, and there would be no need to risk much of anything if you weren't curious about the rewards of doing so. Curious people are also inherently humble, because you can't be curious and knowledgeable at the same time. Best of all, curiosity is a conscious choice. Like work ethic, or kindness, or patience, curiosity is a quality we can all choose to develop. In other words, it's important to be educated, but it's critical to be curious.

CHARLES PAYNE

What role do you believe education plays in shaping a person's life, particularly in imparting values among our youth to become productive members of society? What are some effective ways for individuals to develop new skills or pursue further education outside of traditional academic settings?

Education is okay, but learning is everything. As a teenager, I made a vow to myself to read and learn something new every single day, and I've kept that promise. No knowledge is useless or trivial. My secret is every answer should trigger new questions. There are so many online courses for every subject imaginable. I took a few courses at the New School to learn to write scripts. I write now for my show and my clients and use those skills every day.

BILL HEMMER

What's one essential piece of career advice you'd offer to recent graduates? For example, asking the best question helped make a big difference in your life.

So many of us want to jump on that road to the career we have chosen. And I think that is very important. Oftentimes those who pick a path—whatever the path—you will find yourself years ahead of most of your colleagues. But the one essential piece of advice is this: take the time to experience the world. You won't get a better education.

PATTI CALLAHAN HENRY

When did you realize that you could write novels—what did that feel like?

I was a reader before I was a writer, and I believe that the hints of who we might become are hidden in the things we loved as children. And I loved story. The worlds of *Charlotte's*

Web and *Little House on the Prairie* were alive to me. The power of story and myth resides in its ability to tell us a deeper truth, deeper than the rational mind, pre-rational if you will. We are made for story—it is how we create meaning of what seems meaningless and sense of the senseless. I didn't realize these truths when I was a child—I merely understood that reading nourished something in me that nothing else could.

Then one day, in my midthirties when I was a pediatric clinical nurse specialist, I was playing doll house with my five-year-old daughter, Meagan, when I asked her, "What do you want to be when you grow up?" And she answered, "A writer of books." Her answer, one born of our only time alone with two little brothers pulling at me, hit me in the solar plexus. It took my breath away and I answered, "That's what I want to be when I grow up."

Then she informed me that I was already grown-up. So I signed up for writing classes at our local university the next day. I wanted to write one book, to prove I could do the thing that sustained me for all my life, and that was nineteen novels ago.

MIKE ROWE

Trade schools aren't given enough importance in our education system, as you've helped us open our eyes to. How quickly is that perception changing?

It's changing, but not fast enough. Trade schools have been considered subordinate to universities for the same reason plumbers and electricians have been considered subordinate to doctors and bankers. Stigmas, stereotypes, myths, and misperceptions have kept a whole generation of kids from exploring a career in the trades, and those misperceptions are reinforced every day by a society that still believes the best path for most people is a four-year degree. It takes time to change those attitudes, and I'm happy to say the needle is moving in the right direction. Trade school enrollments are actually up, for the first time in decades, and university enrollments are down.

This is happening in part because organizations like mikeroweWORKS (shameless plug!) are challenging the stereotypical portrayals of vocational careers with real-world examples of skilled tradespeople who are living happy, prosperous, well-balanced lives. But it's also happening because Gen Z is looking hard at the cost of a four-year degree and saying "no thanks."

SALENA ZITO

You know the working-class history of Pennsylvania better than just about anyone. In your experience, what do you believe are the most valuable skills or qualities that blue-collar workers can develop to excel in their roles and advance in their careers?

My family on my mother's side, both the Scots and Germans, has been in Pennsylvania since 1632. My father's parents immigrated to the United States from Italy in 1900. What both sides of my family shared in common with an exception of a few was that we're all from working-class stock.

It is almost all I knew growing up—not just my family, but my neighbors and the parents of the kids I went to school with almost all exclusively worked with their hands or owned small businesses like grocery stores.

Their idea of advancing their careers often centered on

strengthening their work ethic—it was a point of pride to come home and have done the best you could have in that one day and to try to top that the next day.

When you as a community see your value as the purpose you bring to your profession—whether it is running a landscaping business or working at a drill site or a coal mine, or keeping your little grocery store stocked or your barbershop humming—that to them is the best way to excel in their work.

JOHNNY JOEY JONES

What inspired you to pursue a career in the military, and how did you know it was the right fit for you?

Growing up, my family wasn't overly patriotic. That's not to say they weren't proud Americans, just more so proud Georgians. Honestly, before September 11, 2001, you were more likely to see a Georgia flag flying than Ole Glory around the northwest Georgia mountains.

I like to say, "If my family were involved in public service . . . it was in orange jumpsuits on the side of the road because they had too much fun the weekend before."

By the time I got to my junior year of high school (2003) I had older friends I'd played football with graduate, join the Army, go to war, and return home to tell us about it. It was inspiring, but not exactly moving me in that direction.

My two best friends, Keith and Chris, both had dads who were career military. Keith's dad was active-duty Air Force stationed in Arkansas and we didn't see him much. But his uncle had been a Marine and Keith always wanted to become a Marine. Chris's dad enlisted in the Marine Corps in college and went on to become a commissioned officer in the Reserves. He was a coach and teacher at our middle school and had deployed to Desert Storm. He was a little "larger than life" and incredibly proud of his service as a Marine. It was always evident that Chris would join the Marine Corps.

So, by our graduation, things started to come together for Chris. He earned a baseball and Army ROTC scholarship to North Georgia College. Keith and I enrolled in the local community college. Keith worked manual labor for his uncle and I worked in the local carpet mills through the week and laying brick and block with my dad on the weekends.

Things finally came to a head when my habitual bad decisions caught up to me. First, my longtime girlfriend, who was still in her senior year of high school, broke up with me because I was always working or hanging out with my friends. Then another pair of friends I'd made were just bad dudes and I got into a heated argument and fight with one of them that left stitches in my forehead. Lastly, I dropped completely out of college to work a first-shift job. At that point Keith intervened. He had been talking to a Marine Corps recruiter and took me to see him.

After the first visit, I was signed up. Keith signed up with me but failed the one test you can't fail—the one you retake in a month to get it "out of your system." So my two best friends dropped me off at the recruiter station on April 24th, 2005, and off I went to the Marine Corps. Keith joined the Army a few months later and Chris, not to be outdone, joined the Marine Corps Reserves the following spring semester.

TREY GOWDY

In your book, Start, Stay, or Leave: The Art of Decision Making, *I thought the phrase you wrote—"Consult your dreams with wisdom"—was brilliant. With that in mind, what advice can you share on how to balance dreaming big and setting goals with also being realistic and knowing when to adjust?*

Separate what is possible from what is practical and understand it's okay to compartmentalize life to some degree. Dreams are just that, dreams. I dream of playing in a Senior Tour golf tournament. It drives me to work on my golf game to constantly practice, even though in reality the chances of me playing in anything other than a tournament at my local golf club are small.

I dream of writing a miniseries like *True Detective* season one. It gives me something to think about, work toward, a reason to be creative. In reality, it likely won't happen. So, what amount of time do I allow dreams to consume my life versus more practical aspects of life like putting on my makeup for an appearance on a news show?

That is where the wisdom comes in. Knowing how and when and where to allow those dreams to dominate. In addition to, but never at the expense of the so-called real world, at least until your dreams and the real world become one.

Dreams are just that: long-shot goals, best-case scenarios, a trip down nostalgia lane or to "what-if" park. There is nothing in the world wrong with doing any of that—and lots of things are right about it. It's just when the lunch hour is over, it's time to get back to practicing law, or teaching, or selling whatever you sell. And when the evening comes, you can slip back into your dreams.

I played catch with a young man who was subletting from me during the summer of our bar exam preparation. He wanted to don his catcher's mask and mitt and have me pitch to him during afternoon breaks from study. For about thirty minutes he was a major-league catcher. For the rest of the day he was a law student trying to figure out the rule against perpetuities. Both can coexist.

One way to look at it would be like driving a car: work is where we are headed, our destination, if you will, while dreams provide the music we listen to along the way.

SANDRA SMITH

You ran track and field while an undergraduate at Louisiana State University (geaux Tigers!) . . . can you share some values you learned from being a collegiate athlete and how they have translated into your professional career? Specifically, what lessons from your athletic experience have you found vital for success in your current work?

The values I learned as a college athlete are toughness and commitment. Both have been vital to my success. I think about our grueling twice-a-day, six-day-a-week workouts in the hot Louisiana sun and realize just how tough it made me. And oh my, the commitment. Waking up hours before my nonathlete friends each day was tough, but over time I became proud of my dedication.

Even on Sundays in Baton Rouge, we would board a bus before sunrise and drive to the Louisiana-Mississippi border for our weekly "long runs." As the sun rose, we would break through spiderwebs running along narrow dirt trails, spooking animals from abandoned fields as we'd go. Running silently with my teammates, while unspoken, we felt our strength and toughness grow.

Most importantly, we learned to exceed the limits we had placed upon ourselves. It's only now that I look back fondly on those days and say, "That was fun!" I wish someone would have told me!

Being a college athlete taught me so much. But most of all, it taught me that we are only as tough and committed as we push ourselves to be.

That toughness and commitment has played a role in every single day of my career. From pushing my way across busy trading floors to cover breaking financial news, to tracking down Bernie Madoff as he fled Ponzi scheme allegations, reporting live from banks all over the country as the financial crisis hit, preparing around the clock to moderate two primary presidential debates, launching new shows, interviewing Supreme Court justices, presidents, vice presidents, and beyond. I am thankful for all of it, and I owe it to the toughness forged on those long runs under the Louisiana sun.

LAWRENCE JONES

When you were young, you wanted to pursue a career in law enforcement. However, as you grew older, your dreams shifted. Could you share the journey of how your aspirations evolved and what prompted you to change your career path?

Growing up, I was a police and fire explorer and so I always had a passion to help change perception of law enforcement. As I grew older I got involved in politics and that dream evolved into wanting to be a lawyer.

I eventually fell into the TV business. It was never a

dream of mine, but I never experienced such excitement since I played basketball when I was younger. But I never lost that passion for law enforcement. I now have a unique opportunity to help train military and law enforcement K9 dogs. It's my way of serving still.

JIMMY FAILLA

Can a hobby evolve into a viable career, and if so, what steps can you take to turn your passion into your work? What about if your career goal doesn't pay at first? What advice would you give to someone who feels pressured to pursue a career path that aligns with societal expectations rather than their true interests?

I am living proof that a hobby can absolutely evolve into a career. But I should warn you that while many people find my story inspiring, it quickly becomes a cautionary tale once you see how I dress on TV.

But let's Defund the Fashion Police for a second and break this down.

The key to making your hobby a career is to work like it already is. So the thing I tell ambitious hobbyists in every field is to model their plan of attack after the old phrase, "Dress for the job you want."

I've loved that mantra my whole life, although to this day I'm still not sure how it applies to strippers.

As for the clothing-friendly industries, the thinking goes that entry-level employees who hope to land in management should carry themselves with the polish and professionalism of someone who's already there because it demonstrates a level of seriousness that puts you on the radar of people who can help you.

This totally carries over to developing a commercial market for your hobby: If you hone your skills with the intensity of someone who's already doing it full time, that is, *"work* for the job you want," all those unpaid hours will expedite the process of getting better at what you do. What you'll notice over time is that what starts out as friends telling their friends you're really good will morph into customers telling customers. This only happens when you make "quality" your brand, which requires a ton of sweat equity but will ultimately create all the marketing needed to get where you wanna go.

The bad news is that you're not going to be able to pay the bills out of the gate. The good news is that neither could *anyone else* who's ever made it big in whatever field you pursue. Larry David was a limo driver before he got good enough to write *Seinfeld* and *Curb Your Enthusiasm.* Harrison Ford was a carpenter before he landed the Han Solo role in *Star Wars.*

In showbiz they're known as "survival gigs" because they keep the lights on in your apartment so you can stay up late at night chasing that dream of yours. And as daunting as it might sound to put in those extra hours, the truth is you won't feel most of them because there is nothing more invigorating than "going for it in life."

When I was a New York City cabdriver I had to drive my taxi from 5 a.m. to 5 p.m. before I could do stand-up in whatever opium den I was booked in that night. Of course, it's not enough for a comic to simply perform, you need to write material. So every day I would set my alarm at 3 a.m. and meet my writing partner Dean Imperial at 3:30 to write jokes for an hour before I headed down to the taxi garage to get cut off and honked at for the next twelve. As crazy as it sounds, I did this six days a week because I wanted this thing I've now achieved so badly that I never once felt the punches I was taking in my taxi. Although there are days when I'm pretty sure I still have a contact high from some of the passengers.

Point being, if you want to be a hobbyist who "goes pro" you've *really* gotta want it. And while you might not gain the short-term approval of the people who urged you to pursue a more traditional career path, you'll always have the long-term validation that comes from knowing you were part of that small minority who had the guts to get in the ring and slug it out.

The pursuit *is* the success!

Because win, lose, or draw, you wrote your own story in life. Hopefully it involves fewer hobbits and time travelers than mine.

TREY GOWDY

In your book, you encouraged readers to "let fear ride in the passenger seat." It's a powerful concept—especially given how pervasive anxiety is in our daily lives. Could you expand on how one can harness fear as a driving force rather than allowing it to hold you back?

Fear debilitates us. It cripples us. It paralyzes our ability to see things rationally. Fear must be confronted. It must be conquered. And ultimately converted into simply caution, which is actually quite good for us. We must distinguish between fear and caution. That is job one.

To accomplish that we must first be honest with ourselves, which leads me to a side point. You must be brutally honest about what it is precisely we are fearful of: Rejection?

Being exposed? Failure? Success? (Yes, some people are afraid of succeeding.)

Logic beats fear. Playing the probabilities rather than the possibilities. We must train our minds to play the numbers. Yes, there is a chance something awful will happen if we do X, Y, or Z. There's a chance something awful will happen if we don't do anything. There's always a chance.

But do you have a plan for coping, managing, surviving even if the worst does happen? That's how I conquered fear. The chances of me being kidnapped delivering newspapers was small. The chances of my parents leaving me at a store (my mom at least) were small. The chances of me finishing last in law school or not getting anything right on the bar exam were small. And even if the worst did happen, I could conjure a plan for overcoming it.

The only thing we really cannot bounce back from is a life squandered when we reflect back on it.

DR. MARK SHRIME

Do you have any tips for people feeling pressured by family, friends, or trends to pick a particular professional path?

Absolutely. It goes without saying that this is your career, your professional path. Although friends, family, or even trends will have a say in it, you're going to be the one waking up every morning to do the thing. You'll be the one working the weekends to meet that deadline, treat that patient, write that book. Family pressure, the approval of friends, none of those will sustain you in the long run. All this is to say, your career choice can only, finally, be yours.

One other thing: When people who love you give advice, that advice always comes from a place of wanting to see you succeed. You can rely on that. You can also rely on the fact that the advice comes from *their* lived experience, from how *they* succeeded. When I was in the middle of deciding to take a year off to work on Mercy Ships for the first time in 2008, basically everyone told me not to do it! And that wasn't because they didn't care about me, didn't want me to succeed. It was because the path *they* walked, the path that they succeeded very well at, did not include time off to work on a hospital ship. They could see all its dangers and wanted to protect me from it.

They wanted me to succeed; they just had limited lived experience of people succeeding in nontraditional paths. So, for them, the right path to success was the traditional one.

JOHN ROBERTS

You told me that at one point you wanted to study medicine—and that's served you well as a journalist. Prior to joining Fox, you were once chief medical correspondent at CBS News. How did your career ambitions evolve over time—and you ended up on the path to a successful career in journalism?

I was sure that I wanted to go into medicine. Biology was my strongest subject, and I had an innate fascination with the function of life. I was also intrigued by the practice of medicine. As a child, I had several illnesses and severe allergies that took me to my local physician once a week. I was mesmerized by the instruments in his office—from the syringes and otoscope to the dispenser that soaked cotton balls in alcohol.

As I went through my teenage years though, my interests

began to turn. I was a huge fan of Top 40 AM radio and was constantly listening to 1050 CHUM Toronto. At one point Wolfman Jack was even a part of their DJ lineup. Radio didn't get any better than that, and I thought to myself, "Wouldn't it be amazing to be a part of that magic?"

In college I was majoring in science, but the campus radio station was singing its siren song. I found myself spending more time "on the air" than in my labs. I started to weigh my career choices and decided that because I was two years younger than most of my peers (I started school early and skipped a grade) I could give myself a two-year window to achieve my radio dreams. If it didn't work out, I could go into medicine with other students my age.

After interning at the local cable access channel (hosting an afternoon music show), I wrote letters to every small radio station within two hundred miles of Toronto. A couple answered back and asked me to come in to cut an audition tape. One of them, CFOS in Owen Sound, Ontario, liked my tape and hired me. But it wasn't to be a DJ—it was to be a newsman. I still wanted to spin records for a living, but as I moved up through the business, stations kept putting me in the news department.

Eventually I did realize my dream and became a Top 40 DJ at 1050 CHUM. I got there in two years, right on schedule. Now what?

As it happens, fate laid out the path for me. CHUM was expanding and bought a local television station, City TV. The station wanted to launch a sort of "*Rolling Stone* for TV" show and signed me up to do it. *The New Music* broke all kinds of new ground and paved the way for Canada's music channel, MUCH Music (an anagram of CHUM). I was one of the inaugural VJs, along with singer/songwriter Christopher Ward, whose music I had been playing on CHUM.

I knew that music was a young person's game (never thinking that the Rolling Stones would still be doing it at age eighty), so I told the station president that I would give two years to the launch of MUCH, but in return, at the end of that commitment, I wanted to move back into news.

City TV led to my first job in the U.S., at the newly acquired CBS-owned-and-operated WCIX (now WFOR) in Miami. From there I went back to Canada for a brief stint doing CTV's morning show, then back to New York with CBS Network. There was another five years at CNN, then I finally found my lifelong home at Fox. It really is an amazing place, with a sense of camaraderie that I have not experienced since those early days in music television, and I intend to stay as long as they will have me.

JIMMY FAILLA

What are your natural talents? How does one discover their own natural talents?

The way to identify your natural talents is to look at the tasks in your day-to-day life and notice the things you do effortlessly. It could be how you cook or how you communicate with colleagues.

Maybe it's training your pets or fixing things that get broken around the house because you're *bad* at training your pets?

The point is we're all way better at some things than others. These are the areas where you'll find the type of professional work that will bring you personal joy and the good news is we all have *something* that makes us perfect for a particular industry.

Even if you're spectacularly lazy and you only seem good at wasting money, there's a career path for you in *Congress*.

ANDREA ARAGON

How did you think about what you wanted to do for a career when you were growing up in Rocky Ford, Colorado? Did it change over time?

As a small-town girl growing up in a farming town in southeast Colorado, I dreamed of having the glamorous life of a television news reporter. It was the farthest thing from what I saw all around me. I felt certain I did not want a boring job behind a desk. Rather, I wanted excitement, travel, and who doesn't want their face on TV when they're a kid?

This dream suited my academic talents, which were more geared toward public speaking, writing, reading, and communication skills. I continued on this path once I entered college, and I loved it. As I broadened my studies, I found that I could use these skills in just about anything. Over thirty years later, I have found myself in a very fulfilling career as a leader in the nonprofit sector.

Never would I have believed my path would have led me to serve as a tenacious fundraiser, community connector, and cheerleader for the underserved. While it still surprises me, I would not want it any other way. I know now that I'm exactly where I should be.

Be open to where your skills take you, and you could be pleasantly surprised.

DR. MARK SHRIME

What would you tell young people who aren't sure what they want to do? Is dedicating a year or two to a volunteer effort something that you'd recommend? (I do! I wish I could have done it or even known about it!)

Yes, yes, yes! There's less of a stigma around taking time off these days than there was twenty years ago—but there's still some. What will employers think of you? Do you want your CV to look like you're just gadding about?

Can you think of any single religious tradition that *doesn't* advocate taking time away, recentering, regrouping, taking a Sabbath, etc.? I suspect that's because we're not designed to go from one thing to the next to the next until we retire or burn out.

Take some time to do something for others and you'll be surprised at the clarity you'll get about the things you need to do next for yourself.

HAROLD FORD JR.

Deciding to run for public office—in your case the House and the Senate—is a big deal. How did you wrestle with all the different pros and cons to make the decision to go for it? Looking back, would you do anything differently knowing what you know now?

I grew up in and around politics and, most important, people who were committed to public service. My father, aunts, and uncles were all active in politics and the community we lived and loved—some were elected officeholders. They taught me that an elected office is a privilege to hold; to respect all of my constituents, not just those who voted for me; and to try and do the right thing by people all of the time. I'm old-fashioned because to me all of that means I should always be trying to solve problems. Too many people entering politics today do it for exactly the wrong reasons. It's about their importance, not, as I was taught, the people they were elected to serve.

And I wouldn't change a thing because I can't. In general, I don't think that way at all about life. I recently heard the women's basketball coach at Duke counseled her players that life is a constant exercise in handling hard better. I think she's right.

TYRUS

You overcame many obstacles to get where you are today. (Read Tyrus's books, folks—you'll love them!) Do you believe that everyone has it in them, somewhere, to find what it takes to improve their lot in life? What made you so resilient?

Do I think everyone has it in them? No, I do not, to be perfectly honest. You have to face rock bottom alone. Just you and your reflection. Owning your own shortcomings, accepting why you failed and what you're going to change about yourself to be better. There are too many easy outs for people today. Unfortunately, more people look to blame others for their setbacks . . . and look to be given opportunities rather than earn them. But there are enough special people from all walks of life that are not afraid to fail in fighting their way to a better life. . . .

JOHN ROBERTS

Why is it valuable to view job opportunities as learning experiences, even if they don't align perfectly with your initial career aspirations?

Summer jobs in my teenage years taught me a lot about what I didn't want to do. I sold subscriptions for a local newspaper. Built construction loads at a lumber yard. Ran a car wash. Drove a forklift truck in a factory that made Volkswagen mufflers, and kept parts inventory at a chemical company. All of those jobs gave me a lot of experience in understanding how things work. If my local car wash broke down, I could probably help them fix it. I can also instantly spot the difference in grades of lumber (an important talent when building a deck). It was a lot of manual labor too, and I have always liked working with my hands.

But every day that I was working those jobs, I kept dreaming about what I really wanted to do. None of my co-workers could understand why I would take such a flier. Why not just stay where it's safe and you get a steady paycheck? I have never played it "safe." You'll never get to the top of the mountain if you don't risk falling off a cliff.

PETER MCMAHON

You received an excellent education in the United Kingdom, and you were blessed with a strong upbringing. What are the most important values your parents and grandparents and teachers and coaches instilled in you?

My father was a military man and always insisted I stand

up for myself. Once when about ten years old I was punched by an older boy and ran home crying. My father sent me back out and I went up to him and punched him on the nose, making it bleed. I received several more punches but had made my point.

Because my father was posted to Singapore I went to a private boarding school in the U.K., from ages ten through eighteen. While there were of course occasional fights, there was really no bullying and without mommy and daddy to run home to we had to learn to resolve issues ourselves. Not being with them all the time also made me appreciate my parents more and we had a very close relationship.

Something my parents instilled in me was respect for others, whatever their circumstances. I had Chinese, Indian, and Malay friends with whom I played soccer, and we enjoyed soaking up the local culture.

Because the boarding school was expensive and the RAF no longer paid once my parents returned to the U.K., the agreement was that if I stayed at the school, when possible, I would work on the vacations for my personal allowance. So, from pumping gasoline, to furniture removals, to working in a factory and three summers spent working on a farm, I learned the value of hard work, and very importantly that just because someone may not have a lot of educational qualifications doesn't mean they are not smart, and that they are fully deserving of respect. I might have been a pupil at a relatively elite private school, but working on a farm soon taught me how much I didn't know about an awful lot, and brought me right down to earth with a healthy dose of humility.

STUART VARNEY

Was there a moment in your career when you realized "this is what I want to do"?

Yes. There was. It was in San Francisco, and I appeared for the first time on live television with a show about the stock market. I was introduced. The red light went on. And I was hooked. Even though I was very anxious, and my heart was beating fast, it was at that moment that I realized I liked the entertainment and performance aspects of television. I'm not a print guy. I'm a TV guy, and that was the moment I realized it.

GREG GUTFELD

Many young people aren't sure what field to go into after they graduate from high school or college. What do you recommend they do to get started in their careers?

My feeling about careers is not to be too picky. Don't be picky at all, in fact. Do not follow your dreams; follow people. Following your dreams is a terrible idea.

I don't really remember any of my jobs nearly as much as the people who changed my life. And the best way to do that is keep an eye out for people who have what you want. And I don't mean money or status. I mean a sense of calm in what they do. You know "calm" when you see it. I think we started calling it "cool" in the 1950s. But if you're reading this and you're older, remember the first people you were impressed with at work. They were calm, they had a way about them, they made you feel comfortable, and less afraid. In every job, I found that person, or they found me.

I can remember their exact names. If you get your dream job, however, and you're within a group of resentful, or jealous coworkers, that dream will become a nightmare. But even the most mundane entry-level job will become a joy if you seek out the person who has what you want. Which is calm. I had one at Albertsons supermarket, at *Men's Health*, at *Stuff* mag, even now at Fox. Those are the people who will make your career happen. Suddenly you won't have to choose your fate—by some miracle fate chooses you through a series of calm decisions that put you in the right place at the right time.

MIKE ROWE

I once heard you say "you don't want a career, you want the right career." How do you define the difference between a job and a career, and how does this understanding influence your approach to work?

A job is a date. A career is a spouse. Both deserve to be treated with dignity and respect, but trust me, there's a difference.

Chapter 1: Dana's Takeaways

- You don't have to know exactly what to do for a career. Jump right in and see where the opportunities lead you.
- Be mindful of what thrills you and then keep working at having those skills to get the job you want.
- Curiosity is the key to lifelong learning and success.
- Know that everything will be okay, but you have to put in the effort to make it so.

CHAPTER 2

First Rung on the Ladder

(First Job, First Impressions, First Transitions)

I have a love-hate relationship with first opportunities. They're exciting and excruciating at the same time.

First day of school, first kiss, first trip abroad, first dropping off of your puppy at doggy daycare, first recital, first dance class, first . . . well, life is all about having many firsts.

And while I love the anticipation of something new, I'm hesitant to peer around the corners, because something always goes wrong at some point the first time you do it.

Here's the good news: no one expects you to be perfect on the first day of anything—especially your first job.

Here's a great icebreaker at a networking event or when a conversation gets stuck: ask someone how they made their first dollar.

I have a friend who painted houses for his first job. One day he reached into a gutter and found a hornet's nest. He wasn't wearing gloves. He scrambled down the ladder from the shock but jumped when he was halfway down, landing on his back. He suffered from the stings and bruises simultaneously. He didn't paint houses for long, though. Many years later, he ended up being my dentist (Dr. Tim Chase of Smiles NY, everybody!).

Sometimes it's important to do a weird job just to cross it off the list. Another friend was paying off his medical school student loans and took a side job sewing snaps onto the scalps of bald men, onto which hair pieces were affixed. The original hair plugs! He's now a renowned family doctor in South Carolina.

My husband, Peter, had many odd jobs growing up in the United Kingdom, as his father was in the Royal Air Force. He picked fruit, worked on a farm mucking out the stalls, and eventually bartended in a pub in Blackpool, England. Yet some of his best stories—and skills—come from when he sold stereo equipment in Germany at the British commissary. He and his friends lived in a boardinghouse and got up to a lot of no good. But it set him up for a wonderful career in international sales and marketing—and he made lifelong friends of his coworkers.

If you kick off a conversation about first jobs, that will naturally lead you to the next question: Then how did you find yourself working in your current field? Having these discussions expands your knowledge about how someone's hard work led to their lucky break, or how someone started off thinking they would be a professional hockey player and ended up writing hit country songs instead.

Or how someone got on an airplane one day, met the love of her life, and dropped everything to move to another country to be with him. (Hi, that's me.)

Like a lot of my friends, my first job was babysitting. I also was a telemarketer for a while. That was a hard job for me. Cold-calling people to ask if they wanted to buy a piece of exercise equipment was embarrassing and humbling. Though at the time (sigh, this may have happened in the twentieth century) it is amazing how many people used to like to talk on the phone. I made some good money in that job. And we had some laughs. My coworkers and I would crack up about some of the folks' names—"Harry Whitehead"? Did his parents even think about how that would be taken by others? Poor kid—imagine his life on the playground! (By the way, this is the kind of humor we resort to during the commercial breaks of *The Five*. We don't air it because we . . . can't.)

The job I really loved was waiting tables. It is tough, and I'm just grateful for all I learned there. I try to be supernice to telemarketers and waiters. (By the way, always double the tip at breakfast—morning customers are so demanding with their eggs this way and their coffee just so, and on and on. These people deserve more for putting up with us!)

In college, while I was a waitress at Café del Rio, I also worked weekend overnights as a country music DJ. I had no idea what I was doing. I remember introducing my first song like this:

"And here's Tracy Lawrence with her new song . . ."

And then *he* started singing.

Mortified, I kept going. Years later when I filled in on *Fox & Friends*, the producers surprised me with a call from Tracy himself. I will always love his songs! *Find Out Who Your Friends Are*—add that album to your list!

After working as a local news reporter for a short time, I realized I didn't want it. I couldn't see how you got ahead.

I took a detour and ended up working as a staff assistant on Capitol Hill, answering phones for a congressman from Colorado. It was pretty boring as I just took messages and passed them along. My favorite assignment was giving Capitol Hill tours to constituents in town for visits. It got me away from my desk, plus I learned a lot of Capitol history.

A couple of weeks into that job in the early fall of 1995, the new Colorado Avalanche team was coming to D.C. to play the Washington Capitals. I knew nothing about hockey (does this surprise you?). But Coors Brewing Company was buying tickets and providing a bus for anyone from Colorado who wanted to go. I didn't have many friends yet, but my office mates urged me to go along, so I did.

That decision changed the course of my life.

How?

Well, I sat next to Tim Rutten—a great man who was working for Oregon senator Mark Hatfield when we met. We got to talking, and he asked me what I wanted to do in Washington. I said I'd love to work my way up to being a House press secretary one day (I didn't say *White* House).

Sure enough, Tim knew that another Colorado congressman needed a new press secretary. I couldn't possibly apply; I just took this other job.

"That would be wrong," I said.

He said, "You have no idea how this works."

By Monday, Tim had me meet the woman I'd replace if I got the job and, well, the rest is history.

That's how going to a professional hockey game led me to being the cohost of *The Five* and co-anchor of *America's Newsroom*. Easy, straight path, right? Who knew!

Speaking of *America's Newsroom*, my first day there on that show, January 18, 2021, didn't go very smoothly.

I was so uncomfortable walking to the studio. The show has a very early start time, and I had rushed to be as prepared as possible. I keep my work clothes at the office, so I changed from my leggings and boots into a dress and heels. I wobbled down from the twenty-first to the twelfth floor.

I wondered if I was sick; I couldn't manage to walk very well. I got about halfway down the hall to where the hair and makeup team was waiting for me when I looked down and realized that in my haste to get there, I'd put my shoes on the wrong feet.

Great start, Dana. Get it together! (Jesse Watters wasn't the first to use that phrase.)

I stopped, took a deep breath, and switched out my shoes. Then, shoulders back, with a straight gait, I walked calmly to where I needed to be.

It was a good reminder that no matter how much professional success we've had, or how old we are, firsts are still firsts. And making a good first impression and enjoying the learning honeymoon of a new job are part of the joy of our journeys.

Next up, read some of the best stories about firsts and see what you can learn about your own path. Just make sure your shoes are on the right feet before you turn this page.

AINSLEY EARHARDT

What can you tell people about how to handle a change in career plans when they're first starting out? For example, you think you want to pursue one career but then you realize, wait, maybe that isn't for me.

My best advice about changing careers is . . . do it if you aren't happy. You have one life and you will be working in your profession for a very long time. Find your passion and your happiness in your career. If you don't have a passion for the profession you thought you wanted, it's never too late to change course. But, the earlier you do it, the better . . . considering it might take decades to get to the top.

I thought I wanted to be an orthodontist. I worked for Dr. Richard Boyd in high school for four years. Then when I went to college I worked for a different orthodontist my freshman and sophomore years. It was then, when I realized I could *not* see myself working as an orthodontist for the rest of my life. I would have had a fun job (working with young patients) and would have had a nice practice with few emergencies and a good salary. But I didn't love it and the chemistry classes were brutal for me. Therefore, I said many prayers and started looking at other options.

The Journalism School at the University of South Carolina was very well-known and a woman at my home church asked if I wanted to take a tour and meet with her friend who was a professor at the school. I did, applied, was accepted, and decided to change majors and schools. It was the best decision! I knew immediately journalism and broadcasting was my calling. I started over and immediately started doing better in school and felt more confident about my future. I was thriving and enjoyed all of my classes. I had finally found my life's work.

CHARLES PAYNE

What advice would you give recent graduates struggling to find their first job in a competitive market?

As for the first job and the notion of it being the dream job, it's not always possible (in fact, it's rare), but remember, dreams change as well. Don't procrastinate; get a job, and practice being great no matter the task or your passion for the task.

We have singular journeys, but they connect with other journeys already laid out and delivered to you here today. Be your authentic self. Go down roads less traveled. Break down barriers (including those in our own mind). Never stop asking questions.

I'm here because my grandparents were brave. I'm here because my mother and father were brave. I'm here because I want my daughter and granddaughter sitting in the front row to be brave.

JIMMY FAILLA

If you were to give a commencement speech tomorrow, what would be your memorable line or message that you'd hope those lucky graduates before you would hold on to throughout their career?

If I was giving a commencement speech to my high school self, I'd likely include lots of hangover remedies because I was a mess. And don't get me wrong, I got a 4.0 in college, but that was my blood alcohol content.

An old Jamaican woman once told me in the back of my

taxi that "your attitude defines your experience in life." If you have a good attitude, you'll generally have a good time, no matter what challenges life throws at you. If you have a bad attitude life is gonna gobble you up and spit you out, even if things go relatively well.

We all know rich people who are profoundly miserable and poor people that light up every room they walk into. Their disposition is the difference so remember that no matter what career you choose, we're all in the "fun" business. If you die tomorrow, you're gonna wish you had more fun today.

So pursue a life that brings you the most joy and do as much work as you have to in order to pull it off. Don't worry if it takes longer than expected, because you'll always have Instagram to fake it along the way.

MICHELE CHASE

You know all the ins and outs of HR, so let's talk transitions. Is it ever okay to leave a job without giving proper notice? And how do you define proper notice? And how do you leave the job the right way versus the wrong way?

Giving two weeks' notice is an acceptable amount of time to provide an employer *typically*. That's the standard. That is the bare minimum. Particularly earlier in someone's career . . . That's it . . . it's just standard. If you happen to be more senior, like leading teams or a client, being more flexible regarding the timing of your last day to ensure a smoother transition *is appropriate*.

Frankly, if I hire someone who is not being considerate of the people they are leaving by giving at least two weeks' notice or more for someone with leadership responsibility, it does make me question the hire. People remember if you leave making a statement by not providing appropriate notice. It does not mean that your employer can try to lock you in for an *inappropriate* amount of time either. It says a lot about a leader also in how they take your resignation. . . . I find it telling when they flip out or take it personally that an employee has aspirations beyond their current role or wants to try something different and the resignation becomes about the manager. If they flip out, you know you made the right decision.

The way employees leave a company is just as important as to how they enter it. Burning bridges or trying to "take others down" by talking trash is an awful way to be remembered. The world is small, and people check references and also build reputations for themselves, particularly if they stay in one industry. And who knows, you may even want to return to your old company someday or work with a former coworker who took on an exciting role someplace else.

I always suggest taking the high road when leaving a job. We all have choices to make and can choose to leave if we don't feel that we either are a) not growing or b) feeling undervalued or c) just ready for a change, to list a few things. This does not mean that you don't provide constructive feedback to your manager or leadership if necessary. Leaders cannot fix things if they don't know about it. . . . We are not psychic.

MORA NEILSON

You have made remarkable decisions in your life, including in your career. When it comes to transitions, what have you learned about deciding what you want and don't want to do . . . and then making leaps?

Say yes. And always remember you work for people, not companies. When considering a new opportunity, think about the person you are working for, if they will teach you something about yourself or the industry you wouldn't otherwise know. Seek out people who are honest, full of conviction, self-confidence, and know their own sense of self-worth.

BRIAN KILMEADE

What inspired you to transition from sports to a career in radio and television? Could you share a pivotal moment or realization that motivated you to pursue this new direction, despite initial setbacks?

I loved sports and was always intrigued by the news, and over the last twenty years, that reversed itself. What helped me love the news was my passion for history. I was able to gain perspective on world events by knowing about the past—historic rivalries, alliances, economies, presidents. What always bothered me about sports was that I was watching and reporting on other people's exploits, which reminded me that I was not close to being good enough in their sport to ever compete.

STEVE DOOCY

How has your job working in news changed over the years, and what have been the key factors you've used to best prepare for your show each morning for the past twenty-six years?

When I first started in television, there was really just an hour of TV news that our family watched in Kansas. The local news at 6 p.m., followed by the network news at 6:30 p.m. My parents never made it to the late news at 10 p.m., because sometime during *Murder She Wrote*, my dad would start snoring and my mom would say, "Jim, go to bed, you're asleep," to which he responded a thousand times, "I'm not asleep, I'm resting my eyes."

Now of course news is 24/7, and I've gotten up at 3:27 a.m. to do the morning news for thirty years. Unlike my father, who fell asleep in the 8 p.m. hour, I can't stay up that late. I doze off during *General Hospital*.

TREY GOWDY

How do you know when it's the right time to leave a job?

The fact that you are even asking the question is some evidence it might be time. Why are you considering leaving? The work? The people? The challenge? Can you change what is bothering you? Is it your fault you feel unfulfilled? Is it the job you really seek to change or yourself? You must honestly ask if you are simply trying to move, or change, or advance, or escape, and is it really yourself that you are seeking to get away from? I have left jobs for three chief reasons: 1) the work was done; 2) the job had changed, and was no longer what I hoped or dreamed or thought it would be; or 3) the goals of my life were no longer aligned with that job.

As a general rule I tell myself, "When in doubt, don't." It is hard to go back once you leave, so you must have a high degree of certainty as to why. If the workplace environment is abusive or the work is immoral or compromises your ethics, leave immediately. If you feel unchallenged, ask yourself if that is your fault or the job's fault. Where will you go? Is that place really any better? Are you just seeking newness or a real change? The thing about leaving is that the newness always wears off on whatever it is you start. I have striven to leave before everyone else wanted me to. In other words, jump before you are pushed. It's okay to have people miss you, to wonder why you didn't stay a little longer. But you must have a plan before you jump and honestly assess why or what you are leaving. Oftentimes what you seek to leave behind is yourself and that is the thing that will follow you around wherever you go.

DAN BARR

What mistakes do people make early in their careers that could be avoided?

I have seen many young people enter their new situation thinking the world revolves around them . . . and it doesn't. Several years ago, my son graduated from the Navy SEAL BUD/S program and was waiting to report to his new team. He asked an experienced SEAL if he had any advice. The SEAL thought and said, "Be early . . . stay late . . . take out the garbage." (SEAL Team platoon rooms are highly secure and the trash needs to be disposed of separately.) He said that "new guys" don't know anything yet and therefore aren't able to contribute, but that doesn't mean they aren't always being observed by their new teammates.

In my experience, this advice doesn't only apply to Navy SEALS. People are all too happy to help the new guy/gal build out their toolkit. So be early, stay late, and embrace paying your dues. Look at every assignment or task as an opportunity to learn from and help others because, as the SEAL said, you are always being observed.

TOM SHILLUE

How did you make your first dollar?

I'll never forget it—my first lemonade stand. I charged two cents a glass, which was pretty cheap even for the 1970s, but I was going for sales volume over profit. By the end of the day I had about $1.20 in change. It seemed like an impossible sum! I got a huge charge out of it and thus began my lifelong love of entrepreneurialism.

CHARLES PAYNE

How did you make your first dollar? And what did that first job teach you about life and work ethic? What advice would you offer to someone facing adversity or struggling to make ends meet?

I made my first dollar cleaning car windows at stop signs and red lights when I was thirteen years old. But my first job was working in a bodega on 141st and Eighth Ave, owned by Mr. Grady. My mother worked there, and he hired me to stock shelves, etc. Then he took over the space next-door and made it part of his store. Although he knocked down a wall to move between the two locations, he kept a separate entrance.

I ran the whole thing, including working on the register. It was hell. The bullies came in each day and would try to walk out with stuff. I had a crowbar I used as a weapon. The money was great and I drank all the flavored sodas I wanted.

My work ethic came from my father's military discipline, my grandparents working their farm, and the example my mother set. But honestly, I was so grateful for the opportunity.

TOM SHILLUE

Public speaking is a top fear for many Americans. When it comes to first impressions, how you present and carry yourself is very important. I often tell my mentees to find their strong voice. As a comedian, you often have to face this fear head-on. What strategies have you found most helpful for staying calm and owning the room while performing onstage?

Make eye contact. A lot of people think that looking over the heads of the audience is a good way to deal with nerves because you think that seeing faces will make you more nervous—but it won't. When you look over their heads, you're still going to be very aware that you are speaking to a group, but if you look at a face, that group becomes just one person. So, when you speak, do it to one person at a time, and take your time with it—don't dart around from one person to another every other word. Say a few sentences while looking someone in the eyes, then look to another person and say a few more sentences. Each person is an opportunity to help you focus and make you comfortable. Think of it not as a long speech in front of a big crowd, but a series of short conversations with individuals.

BILL HEMMER

At twenty-six, you made a bold decision to quit your job and embark on a yearlong backpacking trip around the world (mostly through third-world countries). You saw an opportunity and took a risk.

How did that experience impact you personally and professionally? Additionally, making such a significant life decision must have required careful consideration. Can you reflect on the process behind making that decision? How did you weigh the pros and cons?

To this day, it was the single most important decision to shape my life. Was it a risk? Yes, but I saw it differently: What was the personal risk if I did not do it? I quit my job, used the fifteen thousand dollars in the bank, and planned the biggest getaway of a lifetime. I was young, but not stupid.

I worked hard to get a job as a sportscaster in my hometown of Cincinnati and wanted to ensure I had something to come back to. Thankfully, I had a boss who saw it the same way. I stayed in contact with the station and the community by sending back video clips for WCPO-TV and newspaper articles, with pictures, to the now-defunct *Cincinnati Post*. That was my insurance. If I catch malaria four months in, I would have a job waiting there.

Here's how I viewed it: all would not be lost. I was gone nearly a year, traveling locally through foreign countries—China, Vietnam, Indonesia, Nepal, India, the Middle East, Eastern Europe, and Russia. What was the ultimate impact of such a decision: when I auditioned for CNN two years later, the travel list on my resume is what landed the job. And all these years later, I get to meet and work with amazing people like Dana Perino!

PETER MCMAHON

What do you recommend to young people about the importance of learning by traveling or even living in another country? How has that helped you professionally and personally?

I have traveled extensively in my life, including living in Singapore as a child, as well as in Germany and Saudi Arabia, and I have conducted business in around seventy countries. Despite the relative ease of travel compared with when I started in the 1980s, it's a big world out there and we can learn a lot from other cultures and attitudes. Their circumstances may be very different, but people in general have the same hopes, fears, and ambitions. They usually have the same pride in their country that we do, no matter how less developed or successful that country may be. Because it wasn't vacation, I was more exposed to some of the real aspects of life in those countries, not just the tourist spots, and it provided me with a greater sense of perspective, including how fortunate I was in my circumstances.

ELISE BITTER

Many people in their twenties and thirties face decision paralysis when it comes to major life choices. How do you help guide clients through that decision-making process smoothly?

Well, smooth is the goal, though it's not always possible! Usually there are lots of bumps along the way. I like to help clients really understand who they are. What are their values and their red lines, and how do they prioritize them? Some people who face "decision paralysis" have low self-esteem, so going through this exercise can help build confidence.

Then I focus on motivation. Are they making this decision for validation from someone else, or is it their own desire to strive for excellence? For example, do they really want to work in investment banking—or does their dad want them to because of the prestige that comes from it?

And then there's this, something we've all heard a thousand times: Nothing in life is perfect. Until we really believe that, we can't truly enjoy anything—work, hobbies, relationships, family time . . . nothing. There is freedom when we finally give up on perfection.

So, by letting go of the anxiety that comes from trying to be perfect, we get more liberty and more joy, even if it's a little uncomfortable along the way.

TREY GOWDY

Can you share some wisdom on decision-making? Young adults often struggle with making significant life decisions, experiencing a huge wave of overwhelm or indecision. What guidance can you offer to help individuals in their twenties and thirties navigate important choices more confidently and effectively?

There are a thousand ways to lead a life of significance and meaning. So, if one path is foreclosed or seems blocked, pick an alternate route. But you have to do something. Do not simply leave the car idling or in neutral. Do not waste time, because if you are in your twenties or thirties, youth and time are two of the most precious resources you have. So, do not squander them but also do not let others define waste or squander for you. Some trips are short and direct—the shortest distance between two points is a straight line; that kind of sentiment. People lower their heads and go as fast as they can to get from point A to B. Others take the scenic route, stop and enjoy the beauty of nature or the new friendships made along the way. Both folks get there in time for their own closing argument, but the trips are vastly different. Where are you going? How quickly? Which route are you taking?

Gather the facts, order them according to what you value in life, assign weight to the factors in your own unique way (I might value climate or access to golf courses whereas you value art and theater), and make a decision knowing that many, perhaps most decisions can be undone and remade and a new path begun. One lateral step or even a setback is not going to dictate the overall outcome of your life. Every one of my heroes lost. You might too. But you can still change the world.

MIKE ROWE

Can you share a time when you had to reassess your definition of success and fulfillment in light of changing priorities or circumstances?

For me, the big moment came in 2001. I had done pretty well, freelancing for twenty-five years. I had a tidy nest egg and a super flexible schedule that allowed me to take my retirement in early installments. Problem was, I wasn't working on anything that really mattered to me. I was still booking my share of commercials, voice-overs, along with lots of acting, writing, and hosting gigs, but it wasn't until I wound up in the sewers of San Francisco, filming a segment for a local TV show, that I stumbled across a format that really excited me.

The actual details of what happened to me in the sewers of San Francisco is too long a story to share here, and probably inappropriate for a book by Dana Perino.

Call it a baptism of sorts—a scatological intervention that led me to conclude that I was a better guest than I was a host.

That simple distinction completely changed the way I

thought about making television and led directly to a show called *Dirty Jobs*. And that show led to a foundation that gave me a reason to think a lot differently about success and fulfillment.

STEVE DOOCY

What career highlight taught you the biggest lesson?

The most important man in my life when I was five (other than my father) was the man I watched one hour every day, Captain Kangaroo. Forty years later, the Captain was on *Fox & Friends* and told me he watched our show all the time. Wait, what? Captain Kangaroo? Are you kidding me?

Dick Van Dyke, Mary Tyler Moore, and a couple of American presidents told me the same thing. I watched and respected them all growing up, and then—they watched me. For a kid who went to school in a one-room schoolhouse on the prairie of Kansas, that is heady stuff.

With my job, I've been around a lot of very famous people. Cooked with the world's greatest chefs. Sang with some of the biggest singers. Hung out with Vegas billionaires. Been to some crazy parties—parties that if you're looking in from the outside, you're dying to be invited.

Kid Rock the singer is a friend (and my neighbor). Imagine his blowout birthday! Actually I was there for one of them, and this is how we celebrated: His mother, Susan, made him a birthday feast of a childhood favorite recipe—Sloppy Joes on potato rolls. And after we sang to him, he blew out the candles on a music-themed sheet cake she got at Costco.

It was a great party. But not what you might expect of Kid Rock.

DAVID BAHNSEN

What question do you think every manager should ask in a job interview?

"Why are you looking for this job?"

The reason I say that is if the person's answer is "I just want a job," that's okay. Put it on the table. Everyone needs a paycheck.

But give people a chance to come into the interview and say, "Oh, because I saw what you did in this venture," or "I read this story about you." If they've done a lot of homework, it's a great discovery question!

BRIAN BRENBERG

What question do you think every manager should ask in a job interview?

"If I spoke with your former colleagues, what would they say is your greatest weakness?"

Self-awareness is a professional superpower. And its absence is kryptonite.

SANDRA SMITH

After beginning your career as a research associate at a financial firm, you then became a trader and later an investment manager. All this before you made the leap into television as an on-air reporter. That being said, you know all about transitions. When contemplating a job transition, how do you know you are ready for a change? What are your thoughts on the importance of securing a new job before resigning from your current position?

I love this question, as it truly defines so much of my life. Working hard at the task at hand and having people take notice is the best way to transition to the next step. I have found that it is best to not force a transition, but to do your best on the task in front of you. The next step will come naturally and the transition will happen.

If you're looking to make a transition, you have already taken your eye off the ball. The best things in my life have happened not because I was looking for them, but because I was prepared. This relates to college, sports, career, husband, and children, absolutely everything! For example, I am often asked about my transition from finance to TV. "How did you do it?" they ask. My answer: I kept my head down—working hard to be the absolute best at my current job. At the time, I had recently been hired away from a hedge fund in New York to work as the only female on an all-male trade desk at an equity firm in Chicago. A sign people were taking notice was when I was asked to represent my company as a spokesperson from the trading floor. I became the new "face of the company" tasked with getting the word out regarding the great job we were doing and the trends we were seeing. This was great for business, but it also became the platform for my transition to broadcast journalism. As I reported live from busy trading pits in Chicago, the calls started pouring in from producers in New York to appear on their programs. Shortly after, calls flowed in to hire me for good. Off I went to explore the world of financial television and what followed. It was a huge challenge but it worked out! Every minute has been worth it, and I look back and am proud of my choice to emphasize long-term evolution over immediate progression.

LAUREN FRITTS

You made a career change after several years in the news business and went to work in political communications. What is your advice for people thinking of making a switch but hesitant for a host of reasons?

I've tried not to look at my career as linear or confined to specific jobs or categories. My journey has been motivated by pursuing what deeply interests me or by really loving the colleagues I would get to work alongside—aligning with my own mission and values. By defining what you truly care about first, you focus your energy on opportunities that guide your career toward more fulfilling work.

When I was working at Fox, I had what I thought was my dream job but then when I met Governor Christie in the greenroom I was inspired by who he was and what he wanted to accomplish. He is an amazing communicator, and I knew I wanted to be part of that in some way. So, without knowing what I didn't know, I made the jump. The job started as one thing and evolved into managing communications, social media, and viral videos for topics like pension benefit reform and the state's budgets, as well as larger events like Hurricane Sandy relief and his 2016 presidential campaign.

Did I have a clue about pension benefit reform or the New Jersey state budget? No. But I quickly learned that I just needed to distill these topics into a fun and understandable way for the people of New Jersey to help them grasp the administration's accomplishments. So I did, and one video even featured Dwayne "The Rock" Johnson—google it, it was a good one.

What I didn't know I learned, and what I could always offer, was my ability to be creative for a larger audience. In the news business, you do that every day.

If you are debating a switch, here are three key areas I would focus on:

1. **Titles Are Temporary, Not Tombstones:** Don't get bogged down by your job title; that's usually just your ego talking. Worrying about titles or job descriptions only gets in the way of what you can achieve. And who knows, you could land yourself at the top.

2. **A Path Is Only a Path Because Someone Did It First:** Choose your journey and pursue the opportunities you want, not what others tell you based on a known career path. Fulfillment comes from doing work you're passionate about and the impact you can make, not the next line on your LinkedIn.

3. **Don't Be Afraid of What You Don't Know:** Someone once said to me, "Men would apply for the king of England if it showed up on a job board." Women often worry about their skills transferring to a new job or not knowing enough for the next job. Remember, every job has unique learning and transferable skills. You bring a unique skill set to whatever you do. And if you don't know something, you can learn it.

HAROLD FORD JR.

What are the qualities that you look for when hiring someone to work for you? And what matters to you when deciding whether someone should be promoted to a bigger job?

How people treat people is the most important consideration for me—after determining if they have the right intellectual skills to fit the job. For example, I like to see how a person interacts over lunch or dinner with our server, the person who seats us and/or the security guard in the building or outside the restaurant. I have little patience for self-importance.

PETER MCMAHON

What is the key for you when hiring someone? The most important skill or attitude?

All the usual suspects: enthusiasm, experience in the field—though not necessarily essential in junior positions, and the right demeanor. Relevant qualifications count to some extent as long as they're tied to experience, i.e., not just theoretical knowledge.

Taking the trouble to dress smartly and present oneself well is a sign of respect for the interviewer who will probably/hopefully be your boss, and an indication of your desire for the job.

Most of the people I have hired have been in sales positions. It's necessary for these folks to demonstrate the ability to talk and interact easily and smoothly, since that's what their job demands. If they're too nervous in an interview, then how would they be trying to close a big deal?

Why do they want to move? Merely being unhappy in their existing position is not enough; they need to really want the new one as a means to progress, not just escape. Dissatisfaction with the current position is common, and while expressing this is okay, candidates should not go off on a rant about their present employer. Dirty laundry should be kept in the laundry basket.

A sense of humor also helps. When being interviewed I was once asked why I was leaving my current company after less than two years. I pointed out the job was not as had been initially described and said, "They told more lies at the interview than I did." My future boss laughed and my irreverent humor worked in my favor.

That being said, it's also important to be honest. One interviewee said he had been the number two salesperson in his big company. I asked, "Why not number one?" And he replied, "Maybe I'm not the best." He certainly turned out to be the best hire I ever made and thirty-five years later we're best friends.

Critical for salespeople is the ability to "close the deal," in other words ask for the job using whatever sales technique is appropriate. I believe that should apply to all positions. If you want the job, then do more than just turning up at the interview and answering questions. Show them you really want the position.

JOHNNY JOEY JONES

For individuals considering joining the military, what factors should they consider to determine if it's the right path for them? What are some common misconceptions about military life, and how would you address them to someone considering enlistment?

I joined in 2005. We were in the middle of a war that would last nearly two more decades and they were desperate to enlist us. I didn't know anything about the Marine Corps when I joined. I was intimidated by my recruiter, and he really made me feel like the Marine Corps was doing me a favor by taking me in, and honestly, I'm glad that's how it was.

You absolutely have more negotiating power now than then. But at the same time, joining the military is a process of deciding to become a part of something bigger than yourself.

You are choosing to be one of many, expendable in so many ways, and lose the "you're so special" narrative that has probably been the norm of your existence thus far. This is a good thing.

Especially for those enlisting out of high school. Remember that the adversity you will be exposed to is so much more valuable in molding you into a successful human than any formal education or well-laid-out plan you could conjure. As we often say in the South, "You don't worry about what you don't know."

In other words, a leap of faith in a direction with the right compass isn't a bad way to go about it. Pick a service and job based on your interest and what you want out if it . . . but consider the worst possible scenario and be comfortable knowing you're going to grow and learn even in that situation.

Give the service you join your first couple of years. Do better than is expected of you, volunteer for everything, take on challenges and learn.

By the time you are up for reenlistment you will either feel like you've made the most of it and are ready to move on or will have earned the opportunity to go do whatever it is you want to do in that service upon reenlistment.

Don't join on some promise you'll learn a specific skill to use in the civilian world after an enlistment. You can go to a trade school instead if that's all you want.

Join to learn how to be the hardest-working, most efficient, more experienced, wiser and better-tested person going into any career you decide after service.

Chapter 2: Dana's Takeaways

- Keep your eyes and ears open in all different types of situations and environments.

- Ask people for their stories—you can learn a lot from other people's experiences.

- Be yourself in interviews. Show your compassion and respect for others—that comes across to future employers.

- Always leave a job on a high note.

CHAPTER 3

A Playbook for Promotion

(Taking Your Career to the Next Level)

I'd be such a better White House press secretary today than I was back then.

I'd be firing on all cylinders because I would take better care of my health and eat more nutritiously to feed my brain; laugh a lot more and show a little more personality in the briefing room; worry less about small annoying things (and reporters!); take my own advice about listening more before I spoke; do something with my hair; and worry less about a lack of sleep (you can sleep when you're dead—or after inauguration).

To be clear, I don't *want* ever to do that job again—but I know how I'd do it better if given the chance to redo those years.

Feeling I'd be better now than then is shared by almost everyone I know—magazine editors, congressmen, police officers, athletes, entrepreneurs, etc. All of us would be better if we could turn back time. Why? Because now we have experience, plus time and distance, to realize how much better we could have been had we known what we know now.

Rewind back to 1995 (yes, we had tapes back then). About four weeks into "Thank you for calling Congressman McInnis's office, this is Dana, how may I help you?" I thought I had learned all I needed to know. I looked around thinking, How am I going to do this for two years? Two years is the time frame I had in mind for how long one was expected to stay in a job before asking for a promotion.

Looking back, I realize that isn't true. Capitol Hill is a place where you can move up quickly, and I did. But I was far from perfect at my job answering phones and greeting constituents in the lobby. There's always something you can do better.

For example, in my job today, if I have a bad show, or something goes wrong while we are live on-air, there's a saying that I love at Fox News: "Well, we get to try it again tomorrow!" Code: we know how to make it better, so let's do that when we meet again. I'm constantly learning in my current role. As soon as that stops, it's a dead end for that career path.

So, I understand that you might feel impatient to get your life underway. I was a young person in a hurry back then. And in *Everything Will Be Okay*, I explain how I worried a lot of my early life away. I don't want you to do the same thing.

Let's agree to be more purposeful and more measured while maintaining high energy and serenity. Easy! I mean, as my Pilates instructor says when asking me to do something that seems impossible, "We try."

Here's the thing. There's no right answer for how long

you should stay in a position before seeking a promotion. While you can't possibly learn everything in a few weeks, I know what it feels like to be stuck and stagnant. The sweet spot is to find a way to move up before you get fed up or even resentful.

Over the years, many mentees have come to me frustrated because they are ready to get to the next level but feel stymied at every pass. Often I'd hear them describe how the job they think they're perfect for requires five to seven years of experience and they only had three. So, their resumes weren't making it to the hiring officer, or the job search algorithm was blocking them from getting in front of the right people. What's to be done? There's some great advice that follows in this chapter for how to get where you need to be for consideration for the job you want.

I've also witnessed all the different ways promotions happen—sometimes it is out of the blue, a huge surprise, and usually a welcome, well-deserved bump up. Other times it is because someone leaves the company or the person in the job you want is promoted, leaving a slot open for you to move up. Still other companies have very rigid promotion structures—you're on a path with clear benchmarks you have to hit in order to get to the next level.

There's no sure way to get to the next level, though three things come to mind:

- **You must work at doing the job you want in addition to the job you have**. Can your manager picture you in that job? Can you fill in for that person when they're on leave or out sick? Do you make your boss's job easier when you're working at that higher level?

- Work with your employer to **make it clear that you have goals to stay with the company and to move up** in the organization. I have found that many managers don't know what their employees' goals are—that's not just on them. You need to speak up and to ask for feedback (and be willing to act on the feedback you get).

- Obsessing over a promotion, or someone else getting promoted before you do, is a surefire way to be miserable in your job and to slow down your moves up the ladder. Instead, **focus on your own skills, build on your knowledge every day, and let go of the worry about being promoted**. It's remarkable how forcing yourself to take your job one day or week at a time can open space where you find yourself with an unexpected opportunity. Put in the work, get on a good path, and the rest almost always will fall into place.

I have one additional rule for people who work for me. I expect them to perform well and to be promotable (and getting them to that kind of position is one of *my* responsibilities).

For example, one of my requirements is that assistants should only be in that position for two years, when they should be urged to go for their next step.

That has not always been the case. My assistant Caroline was wily and wise when she first started in September 2020, knowing that she wanted to stay with me through a general election. I hesitated to say yes, because her potential is sky-high (she's smart as a whip!), and I want her to reach her entire potential. But she really thought it through, and we were able to find additional responsibilities for her that would give her more experience while in that position through the next election cycle. Win-win.

What I really want to discourage is managers who keep their staffers locked in because it's convenient for *them*. Sometimes people love the jobs they're in and they fit their lifestyle and goals—so you can work within that. But as managers we should always be thinking about growing our talent. If there are programs in the organization to help plan careers, take advantage of them. If there's no system, create one or adhere to one you make up on your own. As a friend, mentor, former boss, nothing is more exciting and satisfying than watching my people rise. And if you *don't* do this for people under you, at some point they will blame you for their lack of success (or they won't help *you* when you need it!).

Now, if you're reading this and thinking, I'm ready to be CEO tomorrow, let's go! Just keep one thing in mind: sometimes the promotion isn't always what it's cracked up to be.

I've known salesmen who really wanted to become the sales manager and then want nothing more than to go back to being a salesman. And often for people who love the pace and energy of a campaign, they struggle when after a win they get put into positions of government, where things move at a glacial pace and the bureaucracy gives you fits.

It's good to know that so that you don't feel stuck if you move up. You can either help make the job more productive and satisfying, knowing how you like to be managed . . . or you can decide to move laterally or even go back to something you were doing before. There's freedom here.

You're never stuck.

But you *are* responsible for this next step. Your first transition from your starting job is an important one. You really need to shine.

Keep in mind that it will be different—and so will you. Help your replacement get up to speed.

And then go forth and prosper!

TREY GOWDY

"Why now?" This question is one we've all pondered at different stages of our careers. When it comes to taking the leap to the next level, how can you be sure it's time? What are some key indicators pointing to your readiness to move up?

I don't know that we are ever "sure" or "certain" or "convinced." We are just persuaded by a preponderance of the evidence that moving is warranted or best or needed. It is this magical combination of logic and passion. When I decided to leave my dream job and run for office I made up my mind a thousand times to stay. But there was never peace about staying. There was regret that I failed to venture, failed to try, took the safe and easy way out. So the lack of peace is what led me to leave. Conversely, I wanted to leave a job I enjoyed to pursue the safety and security of a federal magistrate judgeship. But I also did not feel peace. I felt security and predictability but not peace. So I wound up passing that opportunity by.

Different stages of life bring different needs and wants. When we are young we may covet excitement. When we have family we may covet time away from work. When we get older we begin to think about security and legacy. Each stage requires a different analysis. The simplest test is how much time do you spend thinking about leaving or trying new things. How much of your energy is spent simply settling versus striving. I advise young people all the time not to settle, but to strive.

MICHELE CHASE

Let's talk resume tips! How can individuals stand out in a competitive job market? When looking at candidate resumes, what jumps out to you?

Be clear and concise with your resume. Cater your resume to the job you are applying for. There may be some particular strengths or projects that you worked on that will help make your resume pop that show you are staying current in your field of expertise. Or if you're just starting out . . . showing that you've pursued opportunities to help build out the skills you need in order to add value to a team.

If looking at a junior candidate, I really like seeing that they had experience beyond just having internships. Yes, internships are great, but individuals who have worked with the public, say in a restaurant, store, or even at their local public pool lifeguarding. *Or* if they played a team sport, were engaged in clubs, where it wasn't just about them but about a team or community. Those are the resumes that stand out to me.

It's not easy working in an office that has a million different personalities or a demanding boss or clients. The resumes where candidates had to work with the public or engaged in activities where they had to work with others for a common goal, those are the ones that stand out.

For those who are further along in their careers, I look at how many times they may have been promoted at one company. I really like when I see that someone has left a company, only to come back a few years later at a more senior level. Getting back to the point of never leaving poorly and people remember how you leave . . . if they are a "boomerang," I know that they were well respected and likely very good colleagues who people missed when they left. It also shows me that they were able to continue to have a healthy network of former colleagues and hopefully friends.

SANDRA SMITH

What is something that jumps out for you on a resume when you're looking to add someone to your team?

Previous individual accomplishments or success . . . at anything. Being the best at something takes a special combination of skill, determination, and creativity. If that person is inspired by what we do and is eager to learn, that is an awesome combination that can lead to great success.

MORA NEILSON

Right versus wrong: What do you look for in new hires? What stands out to you when you're presented with resumes? Do you call references?

I'm always looking for people who are bold, brave, and

courageous. Excellence takes passion and vulnerability. Vulnerability is one of the most endearing yet underrated qualities in a great business leader or associate.

DAN BARR

What makes a young person's resume stand out to you? Does something adventurous catch your attention?

A few years down the line, a young person's resume will be evaluated largely on the quality of their experiences, rate of progression/advancement, reputation of the organization(s) they are affiliated with, etc. Before that track record has been built out, it is important to try to differentiate oneself from the competition. Interestingly, unusual experiences can often say a lot about a person and can be a way of separating oneself from the pack.

Atypical experiences can provide insights into one's character or sense of initiative or risk tolerance or service. Military service is an obvious example of this and completely speaks for itself. I once interviewed a woman who was part of an all-female boat crew that sailed around the world on a masted clipper ship. In addition to being a really interesting story, I thought it said so much about her team orientation and courage and risk tolerance.

I know a young guy who wanted to pursue a career in sports management. He wanted to become a major-league general manager, and in this pursuit he was able to secure an internship with a Kansas City Royals minor-league affiliate. Part of his duties included having to dress up as a mascot when the regular mascot wasn't available. He had to dress up as a giant celery stalk who would run out onto the field after every home team home run. In addition to being very funny and the topic of great conversation, it showed he had a "whatever it takes" mindset and a sense of humor.

Sometimes, the road less traveled gives great insight into what makes people tick.

LAUREN FRITTS

As an executive you had to hire and fire many people. Was there anything that ever really stuck out to you on a resume, or if someone made it to an interview could it really assure you that they would be a good hire?

The truth is, hiring is hard. The process has become way too drawn-out because we all now seek consensus among too many people for one hire, resulting in a poor experience for both candidates and employers. Sometimes you just need to take a chance and trust your gut. While there is no perfect equation, here are a few things I consider:

1. A clear resume that shows commitment and demonstrates results and impact is crucial. I appreciate seeing that someone has stayed at a company for at least two years. Candidates who highlight their achievements with concrete metrics or examples always catch my eye.

2. The most important factor for me is the conversation during the interview. A candidate's enthusiasm and curiosity about the role and the company are

strong indicators of a good hire. Asking insightful questions and showing a genuine interest in how they could contribute to the team set them apart.

3. Additionally, team fit is crucial; in the interview I do look for signs of adaptability, teamwork, and a positive attitude.

JESSE WATTERS

When you're hiring someone to be a producer on Jesse Watters Primetime, *what are the characteristics you look for (since you did all the jobs leading up to host!)?*

We look for a positive attitude, strong social skills, great work ethic, and attention to detail. It obviously helps if you're a news junkie and follow politics closely as a habit—that way work is fun and comes naturally.

Being a producer is all about execution. Doing the job at a high level consistently and on time without making the same mistake twice. On live television, producer mistakes show up on-air. What you see on the screen, the video, the words, the sound bites, the quality of the programming, the quality of the guests, and especially the editorial shape the storyline. Some mistakes don't show up on-air but still exist. The anchor recognizes them. Trust me.

JEANINE PIRRO

You broke a lot of barriers as a young, female lawyer. What is your advice for young people starting their careers who want to be noticed, promoted, and rewarded for a job well done?

If you are looking to be noticed, promoted, or rewarded for a job well done, your priorities may be in the wrong order, and your supervisors, managers, or bosses will see you as a grandstander. The way to be noticed is to love the job, work at it, and ultimately perfect it. Your focus, drive, and perseverance are what will be noticed. A job well done attracts attention. The star will come to you.

MORA NEILSON

How can individuals best position themselves for promotion? And what do you recommend people do if they feel stuck and that others are being promoted over them? Should they stick it out or make a jump?

Always hold your management accountable. You can't fix what you don't know is broken, so ask for feedback and then action against it. Don't take promotions too personal; often they are outside of your management control. Identify a sponsor within your organization if you can. . . . This is very different than a mentor as a sponsor is someone within a company who is in a position of real authority and power who has a vested interest in you and can help to steward your career.

BILL HEMMER

When it comes to taking your career to the next level, how do you know you're ready? Specifically, after spending years as a field reporter, what signaled to you that you were ready to transition into the anchor chair? What are the key indicators pointing to your readiness to move up?

Generally speaking now, when you're young and just

starting, I'm a big believer in the two-year theory. Generally it takes an individual about two years to master a position. Once that is done, you move to a bigger challenge, again for two years. And then a bigger challenge. For example, if you start working around age twenty-one, you will find yourself ready to make big moves in your late twenties and you'll find the people who employ you have greater trust at that point. Then, arguably you set yourself up to make even bigger moves once you hit thirty. Generally speaking, that's how I see someone progress through their career.

MIKE ROWE

How important is it to be willing to take a risk in life? What can you do to get more confidence so that you're not risk-averse?

It's vital. In life there is no substitute for the willingness to assume a measure of calculated risk. Failure to do so would keep every boat to the harbor, every car in the driveway, and every citizen in his home, in a state of perpetual lockdown. No other virtue can replace the willingness to fail, flounder, or fall flat on your face.

As for confidence, that doesn't always develop as a result of succeeding at something. Oftentimes it develops when you take a risk that doesn't pay off, and then, realizing it's not the end of the world, and trying again.

As clichéd as it is, nothing ventured, nothing gained.

MICHELE CHASE

Should you ever leave a job before you have another job?

Honestly, it's always easier to find a job when you have a

job. You don't want to get into a situation when you are running from something . . . you want to be running *to* something. It seems like every time someone really wants to look for a job, opportunities just don't come up and people start getting concerned or even start questioning how capable they are.

If taking a new job, you want to be thinking about if the job fits your aspirations, if the culture and the people you're meeting with are people you would enjoy working with. . . . When you go into it without a job, the urgency to accept something that may not be right can be a mistake. But know that if you do decide to take a new role that ends up not being the right fit, you can always make a change.

CHARLES PAYNE

Is it ever worth it to take a pay cut to make a career change or transition? As a follow-up, what advice would you offer to someone facing adversity or struggling to make ends meet?

I'm a risk-taker and think it's okay to take a pay cut to make a transition toward your goal(s).

My advice to those who feel they've hit a rut or rock bottom? Never give up. To this day, there are a number of hurdles I cleared, and I'm still not sure how—really on the verge of ruin, getting kicked out of homes and businesses, etc.

So never stop grinding and believing.

JOHNNY JOEY JONES

I can think of few people who know more about facing and overcoming adversity. What advice would you offer to someone who feels like they've hit rock bottom?

Adversity is as dependable as the setting sun. Not if, but when.

But as consistent as adversity is, it always catches up when we least expect it and feel least prepared for it.

Yet that's also when we need it most.

The real key is simply perspective. Bad things are going to happen in our lives whether we prepare for it, try to prevent, it or not. So what's left is a simple choice, a choice made with perspective.

We can't always choose what goes wrong, but we can always chose how we respond to it.

When I lost my legs, I had done everything I could for an entire deployment to not get injured taking bombs apart, yet there I was, laying in a hospital bed, no legs, a right hand that I couldn't feel or move, a tube in my side, and a face full of stitches.

The choices in front of me were simple, stark, and immediate: let the pain and frustration and shame make me an invalid others have to take care of and feel sorry for, or use this moment to do whatever I could to get back on my feet, continue a career, and still be someone others can depend on, respect, and love. The pain and frustration were going to be there either way. I just had to choose to not let it stop me.

From that one easy choice, and humbly accepting help and advice from others, I moved mountains.

Had I never been injured, I might not have ever become the type of guy who could move mountains or knew how. That adversity was a challenge accepted, the pain and fear a process to grow, the limitations merely roadblocks requiring a different path to a new destination. But through it all, I continued to move forward.

That's the key. A day at a time, a goal at a time, a win at a time all add up to a time when we can look back and say, "That wasn't so hard . . . what's next?"

BENJAMIN HALL

When you followed your dream of being a war correspondent, you had several setbacks but incredible adventures. For those feeling like they aren't getting anywhere pursuing their dream, what would you say to them about perseverance?

Perseverance is realizing that you rarely get it right on the first attempt, but that by adapting, being willing to learn, and working hard, you can always find a way of getting there.

I look back and realize that I learnt something from every setback I had. Every border I couldn't cross, every interview I couldn't land, every story I couldn't sell, I went away and learned from each one. And every time something didn't work, I would find what did work, even if it was small, and I would enjoy those, then find areas to improve what didn't.

When things weren't easy, and when I couldn't break through as a journalist, I would go back and change the way in which I was working. I'd change who I was working with, the format I was working in, or when and where I was working. I would see what everyone else was doing, then try to do it my way, not theirs.

But I was also willing to learn from people and accept when I made mistakes, because perseverance is about learning too. It's about asking questions, being open to change, and knowing that you can learn even in the strangest places.

Perseverance is not letting nos affect you. I just kept

knocking on doors, kept meeting people, and kept sending emails, and eventually it worked.

Perhaps most importantly I found it's not just trying to reach a goal; it's about enjoying the journey along the way, both the ups and the downs. Because the journey is far more rewarding than the finish line and I learnt more about myself in the tough times, and in the dangerous moments, than I ever did from the safe ones.

JESSICA TARLOV

What is your advice for people ready to make the next step from entry-level to middle management or beyond? Did you have a sense of when you were ready for such a move?

My journey was a little bit different than most because I stayed in academia for so long and then worked at a small company that didn't follow a traditional promotion structure. That said, I got the "what's next" itch two to three years into my first real job. I then told my boss I was ready for more responsibility and, crucially, could help expand our business.

In a majority of settings, that's the key to moving up: make it worth *their* while. How will you help them win more, make more, expand their reach, and/or make more of a difference? And have a clear plan as to how you'll do it versus just saying it.

Here are three pieces of advice for that ready-to-move-up period that I think really help people to get where they're going:

1. Find a mentor who's really invested in you. There are lots of mentoring programs or people who will

have a passing interest in you and your career. You should find someone for whom your success really matters.

2. Tackle the new skills you'll need to excel in your new role. With each progression, there's a skills challenge and growth opportunity. Don't shy away from it.

3. Don't sell yourself short. Women are more likely to do this than men, and it holds so many of us back. If there's a role that appeals and makes at least 50 percent sense, go for it. What's the worst that could happen? Rejection is healthy and maybe you'll get it!

MICHELE CHASE

If a promotion is out of the question, but you are still eager to transition from your current role . . . could you attain some of what you are seeking in ways other than a promotion? For example, could a lateral move within the organization give you what you want? Or how do I know it's time to consider a new job, a new career, a new company or industry?

If you don't see any opportunity for advancement in your current role, and you want to stay in your current company, pick your head up and look around! There could be potential opportunities to engage on other teams and upskill in different ways—networking with other people outside of your immediate day-to-day colleagues and leaders. If you're proactive and intellectually curious about the business or how other parts work, talking with others and raising your hand to help is a great way to go—and to become known for always being willing to jump in.

If your company is too siloed, and/or others are not open to you engaging on projects or lateral mobility across the company, then I would say it is time to look for something else.

A company's culture could be supportive or stifle any cross-business engagement. If it's culture, then moving to a competitor or parallel industry or job may be the answer. Obviously if you don't like the industry you are working in generally, then you should consider pivoting to a new career.

DIERKS BENTLEY

The music industry is so hard to break into. What lessons have you learned from setbacks or disappointments you've experienced along the way? What advice do you have for coping with rejection?

Like any business, there are so many setbacks in the music industry. One thing that helped me throughout my journey, and still does now, is just keeping expectations low. That doesn't sound very fun, I know! But it really helps for self-preservation. Never expect anything to work out, so it won't hurt as bad when it doesn't.

But the flip side is when something good happens, you really get to celebrate! I will say too that there is a lot of truth to the Garth Brooks song "Unanswered Prayers." Sometimes doors close on you for a reason.

So many times, something didn't work out, some producer didn't come to my writer's rounds, a song didn't do well at radio, I didn't win an award . . . and at the time it was disappointing.

But later on, with the benefit of time, I realized that it was for the best, that something bigger and better was waiting for me.

BRIAN KILMEADE

What were some of the biggest challenges you faced early in your career, and how did you face rejection and overcome it when you were first starting out? (Would love to talk about all the rejection letters you kept!)

The biggest challenge was landing my first real broadcasting job. You need a tape of your work to get a job, and coming out of college, I had almost no tape. At the same time, I was working any and every side job to earn money to make this tape and send it out. I was not getting anywhere, so I decided to launch my own show with my great friend from soccer, Rick Fatscher, and my future wife, Dawn—both of whom were TV majors. We started two shows, *Health Digest* and *Time Out*, and I learned to shoot, edit, and produce. I got sponsors, car service for guests, wardrobe and catering deals, as well as underwriters. Soon I had a lot of tape of me in the studio and in the field, hundreds of connections, and started getting interest from news directors. They could no longer say I didn't have experience, but it was not typical experience. So I started doing stand-up to add more skills and hope to open more doors. The challenge was economic. I had little money, most earned from waitering and health club sales. I set up a system of hunting for jobs, finding advertised want ads, and operating a fail-safe system of follow-up and writing thank-you notes. I kept every rejection letter—there are hundreds—because I thought one day this would make a good story, and now it is.

JIMMY FAILLA

Self-confidence is key when it comes to asking for a promotion. It's also key to thriving in your current role. But life doesn't always go your way. Any tips for building back self-confidence after making a mistake or falling short of yourself?

There's an old saying that "repetition builds confidence" and it applies to both the "build up" moments in your career as well as those soul-crushing rejections where you need to "build back."

The buildup is that period where you establish that you're good enough to make it by doing enough repetitions to make succeeding become second nature. For instance, when I started out in stand-up, doing a five-minute set in front of ten people in a bar on the Lower East Side of Manhattan was the scariest thing in the world. Granted, it's because half of them were usually wanted criminals or junkies looking to score drugs. (I wish I was kidding.)

But the point is, it took a ton of reps to get me past that initial terror of bombing onstage. Over time I've done enough stand-up sets that I can walk on in front of a thousand people with the same relaxed vibe I'd have at dinner with my wife and kid. Technically speaking the stage is probably *more* relaxed because I never have to yell at my audience for not doing their homework.

The challenge comes when you've built up your act to a place where you get a shot at a big career jump and don't get it. This is where you need to "build back" your confidence and the key to doing it is to immerse yourself in your work, because over time, you'll demonstrate the same level of proficiency that got you the big audition to begin with, at which point you'll feel whole again.

Early in my career I auditioned for a Burger King commercial that I truly thought was going to change the world. The hook was that we'd be walking up to an outdoor drive-through in Madison Square Park and placing an order with a guy who would be looking us over and insulting us from behind the glass. Seeing as I loved talking smack and I already looked like I got paid in fast food, I thought I had it in the bag. I was absolutely manic in the two weeks leading up to it and spent at least ten hours a day dreaming about what I'd do with all that "corporate pitchman money" once the checks started rolling in. Unfortunately, when game day came it was pouring. My actual turn at bat came three hours later than it was supposed to, at which point I proceeded to bomb so hard I'm pretty sure Hamas claimed responsibility for my set.

Looking back now, I realize that I absolutely let the rain and the wait time affect my mood in a way that I never would now because being a professional means blocking out everything and getting the job done under any circumstance. Nobody watching you on TV cares if you had a rough commute or you didn't get enough sleep the night before. They tuned in because they expect a level of proficiency from you, and the reason you're in a position to give it to them is because you've persevered through a billion situations like the Battle of Burger King Hill.

And that's where the "build back" repetitions are so vital. Ninety-nine percent of success in every field is the ability to persist through failure. The most successful people you know have all pitched their bosses projects that left them looking more confused than an Amish guy at the Apple Store.

It's at this point that the unsuccessful people go to a bar and the successful people go back to work (after stopping off at the bar in my case).

So to put this in Value Menu terms, which I was supposed to be doing in the park that day, give yourself permission to fail, but never give yourself permission to quit because in the end, we're all in the keep-going business. As long as you do, your confidence will come along for the ride. To my credit, I got back onstage after my quest to conquer Burger King left me drowning in the moat. For that I was rewarded with a dozen more opportunities that I also tanked along the way.

GREG GUTFELD

What did you learn from the setbacks along the way? You were fired a couple of times for pushing the envelope a bit.

The reasons for my firings had nothing to do with the success of the product, until it did. I created the situation where firing was possible. I guess through my actions I decided I needed to be fired. In almost every situation, however, the firing led to a drastic improvement in my career and in my happiness at work. I can't stress that enough—and it's a cliché for a reason: from pain comes reward. Sometimes you don't want to go through the pain because in the obvious immediate sense, it's hard and creates uncertainty. So you stay at the job for comfort—a moat against uncertainty. But life needs a measure of risk or you will be restless and irritable. The introduction of risk (or to put it a better way: adventure) eliminates the time you would allocate for self-generated anxiety. Better to have the anxiety to come from outside, and meet it by "getting your butterflies in formation," than to create anxiety, which is almost always unbeatable (because you have no outside challenges to focus on).

A good piece of advice is to always be moving, literally to a new place—a job or a city. I look back at my career and I am flummoxed at times how I got to this particular stage. But then I do see a pattern: I made my luck by moving to places where there would be more opportunities for luck.

Taking a nonpaying gig at the Huffington Post when it launched seemed unimportant—but that was the place where Fox first noticed me, not heading up magazines like *Men's Health*, *Stuff*, or *Maxim*. That decision—going to a place that threw me in front of new eyeballs—created an opportunity for luck, getting the show *Redeye*. *Redeye* led to *The Five*, *The Five* led to *Gutfeld*, etc.

PATTI CALLAHAN HENRY

Revealing your writing to others is one of the most anxiety-producing moments I've ever gone through. Is it the same for you? How do you manage that fear? And what about the fear of rejection . . . you know after you put your work out there to the world? Have you found ways to manage criticism that don't cripple your creativity?

There is a very particular anxiety in releasing the creative work of our hearts and life. This anxiety carries a different resonance than worries that keep me awake about things in my life that I have no control over. A book's release vibrates with vulnerability. I feel exposed. I don't know if I manage this anxiety as much as I have learned to live with the discomfort, carry it with me like a traveling companion I didn't invite but must tolerate on the journey. There are two choices: putting my work into the world or hiding it because I wake up with my heart beating out of my chest. I choose the latter.

Finding ways to manage rejection and criticism is one of the biggest challenges in a creative career. For answers to this very particular knife edge, I often turn to experts like Rick Rubin, Madeleine L'Engle, and Julia Cameron, to those who remind me over and over that creativity isn't about acceptance, isn't about winning, and isn't a zero-sum game.

Creativity is, for me, a way to understand a world that often seems confusing, and to face the uncertainty, suffering, grace, and mercy of being human. When I remember those truths, the rejection and criticism can only fine-tune my craft.

BILL HEMMER

Your ability to remain cool, calm, and collected amid breaking-news situations is impressive and admirable. What advice would you offer to others facing high-pressure scenarios or crises on how to best approach the situation one step at a time? As well, can you share some tips on how to handle feeling overwhelmed or out of your depth when starting a new job or taking on new responsibilities?

Absolutely one can feel overwhelmed. I don't see it as unhealthy because it can focus the mind. When you're under pressure, work nightmares can be common. Embrace that moment to be a better version of yourself. Rise to the challenge.

I get plenty excited (as family and friends can attest), but I think there's some trigger that tells me: when the temperature gets hot, you better cool down.

I think the best advice I would offer is that no matter the

news one receives, think with a clear head. It will serve you well under stressful times. Maybe I should have been a pilot!

MIKE ROWE

How have you approached learning from failure or setbacks in your professional development journey?

For a long time, I worked as a freelancer in the entertainment business. From the day I turned seventeen, to the day I sold *Dirty Jobs* to the Discovery Channel, I auditioned for over two thousand different gigs, and booked about 20 percent of them, which, believe it or not, is actually pretty good in my industry. But still, my failure rate was about 80 percent over a twenty-five-year period.

The only way to feel good about failing 80 percent of the time is to think differently about what the job really is. For me, that meant seeing every audition not as an opportunity to book a job, but rather as the job itself. Once I saw myself as a professional "auditioner," I stopped feeling discouraged by the ones that didn't lead directly to a paycheck.

TREY GOWDY

Can you share a time when you had to reassess your definition of success and fulfillment in light of changing priorities or circumstances?

I left my "dream" job after less than six years because my "dream" had changed. But in leaving I risked nearly everything. I was a federal prosecutor, which I loved, but the caseload, the workload if you will, had become monotonous and routine. I had tried nearly fifty cases to verdict but most of them were drugs or gun cases. If you really want to do something about violent crime you need to be in the state system, which meant a shift in jobs to becoming a state prosecutor. It was perceived as a step down by some and it came with considerable risk. You see someone else already had that job. He was elected. I had to resign my "dream" job and challenge an entrenched incumbent.

All of my life's priorities were competing against one another. I needed work to provide for our family and I had to quit the federal prosecutor post to even run for district attorney. How would I provide? How would I make money? What would I do if I lost? One thousand times I decided to stay and take the path of least resistance. I decide to settle. But there was no peace.

So, finally I told myself I did not want to die saying what I wish I had done. Or almost did. Or came close to doing. So I ran. Because my idea of success and significance was in the striving, not the winning. It was in the process of trying, not the electoral outcome. I won because I dared to try.

JESSICA TARLOV

Do you have any suggestions for how young staffers can channel their desire for more (responsibility, money, titles, etc.) and their need to really take some time to master skills in their current roles?

Patience really is a virtue and that's never truer than when you're starting out. I'm not suggesting that you curb your drive or desire to move up. Instead, having an understanding that the early years are full of opportunity for growth and skill building that's very hard to access when you're further up the totem pole is a major benefit. Once promoted, you'll be too busy doing other things to get back to the fundamentals, so seize the opportunity!

One of the areas that I think is especially important to work on when you're beginning is your soft skills. Becoming—and then showing off—what a great team player you are, how you use creativity to problem-solve, how you listen to others, and adaptability are all qualities in an employee and future leader that people in senior positions notice. If you play well with others, you will go far. And you can use your colleagues to practice your management skills in small ways like being part of a chain that will help you immeasurably throughout your career.

Being part of a group where you are all working to better your skills, and treating each other with kindness and respect, is a formula for success. There's no need to worry that there won't be opportunity for differentiation if you're working together. Good bosses see everything and what areas you excel in. And always, always keep an eye out for mentors.

LAUREN FRITTS

How important is follow-up after an interview, and what is the right amount of follow-up to stay on the radar but not get annoying?

Follow-up after an interview is very important as it reinforces your interest in the position and keeps you on the hiring manager's radar. A thoughtful thank-you email within twenty-four hours of the interview is essential. In this email, mention specific points from the interview that excited you about the role and reiterate your enthusiasm.

If you haven't heard back within the timeline they provided, remember things can be hectic on their end too but a polite follow-up email a week or two later is appropriate. It's important to strike a balance—show your eagerness without appearing overly persistent. Don't overthink it. Just do it.

PETER MCMAHON

Starting a business is daunting to many—you've done it. What's the key to pushing forward even though the risk feels too high and the rewards can be hard to see . . . until they're there and you're so happy you did it?

I think for anyone starting a business, whether their first or not, it's a dream they want to fulfill, for whatever reason, whether financial reward or just the satisfaction of doing it. And that is an incentive in itself.

To see something grow from an idea, a concept, to the point where it is a viable business is extremely rewarding. It always takes longer and costs more than anticipated, and no matter how smart or experienced you are, there will be surprises and hiccups en route. And it's important not to be blinded by your ambition to the extent that you don't regularly reassess and reevaluate your progress and what is still required (and in some cases it is necessary to call it a day and look for another opportunity). But if you believe in what you are doing and have the right plan, in your heart you are convinced that it will succeed, so that it will be worth it in the end.

TYRUS

How did you learn to manage rejection and to get up off the mat and try again?

Rejection can cripple some people—make them scared

to try again. But for me, rejection was an old friend. I was born with it, molded by it, by the time I was a young man I was comforted by it. But I never accepted rejection. I never accepted "NO!" Every time I was told no you can't, or you don't have it, I would only say to myself "bet" and begin to outwork whoever was put in front of me. Rejection is a great motivator and fuel. And success is the best revenge.

BENJAMIN HALL

After your war injury, you found a well of courage to help you heal and return to your family. Do you believe everyone has that courage inside of them?

One hundred percent. I was amazed at the level of strength I found inside me, strength that I didn't realize was there. Nor did I realize to what degree we can control our fears, control our pain, and dig down to find the drive we need to keep going.

Before I was injured, I had often seen people hurt in war and I wondered how I would react if it happened to me. When it did, I found it easier to handle than I expected, because when you are up against a wall and have to find a way through, you can and you will, because it is in us all. I think it's because in normal life we are weighed down by concerns that aren't real, about things that society dictates, rather than ourselves. When you are going through something of the scale I did, you forget all those, and if you look closely at what you want to achieve, and where you want to go, you will find the extra strength to do it.

It was perhaps natural courage, but it was mainly the ability to channel everything into getting through the tough times. What worked for me, and what I told myself, was that I would go and achieve something new every day, no matter how small it was and no matter how hard it was. That I would walk farther, live more, do extra physio, if only for a few more minutes. Then I would do it longer the following day, and just keep building, and eventually you get where you want to.

So just take one step at a time, enjoy the small victories, and grit through the tough times, because on the other side of hardship there is always something wonderful—joy, family, safety. The harder it is, the greater the reward. Courage isn't about it being easy; it's about realizing that you can get through even the tough times.

And courage comes from flexibility. It doesn't come from being set in your ways or mindset too much. You must be willing to adapt to be truly courageous.

Chapter 3: Dana's Takeaways

- Keep your resume clear and concise.

- Taking tentative and small steps won't get you very far. Lengthen your stride and step boldly or else risk falling behind. Especially as you're working your way up the ladders. High risk leads to high rewards.

- Put yourself fully into the job you have. Try to improve on something every week. Your employer will notice.

- When you feel stuck, realize that you have the power to change that. You can make a move before you get pushed. Make a decision to act, not wait.

- Celebrate success. Don't dwell on disappointment.

CHAPTER 4

Reaching New Heights, Taking On More Responsibility

Let's kick it up a notch.

Once you've had your first job and made your first transition, you've learned a lot—from your achievements and your mistakes. You have an idea of what you want to do and what you would never want to do. You're ready for a lot more responsibility and you want to make some more money.

Now you're ready to kick your career into a higher gear.

Thinking back, my first real move to a higher level was when I transitioned from being a spokesperson at the U.S. Department of Justice to leading communications for the White House Council on Environmental Quality (CEQ).

President Richard M. Nixon created CEQ to coordinate all the energy and environmental issues across the federal government. And there were a lot of them. Everything from the endangered black-footed ferret to greenhouse gases to healthy forests to snowmobiles in national parks.

I had to step up in that job and help the White House press office by taking on any inquiries that dealt with those issues, managing any events that dealt with energy, conservation, or the environment.

There were many times when I had an inkling of what needed to be done, but I really had to stretch myself to learn all I could and be very smart about answering questions from reporters. The media liked trying to trip up President George W. Bush on anything dealing with energy (well, on anything and everything).

I tried to keep my head on straight. One thing that kept me grounded is this story, which I remember fondly. My mom called to ask how the new job was going. I said it was great and that I was learning so much and meeting a lot of people.

I told her that *even Karl Rove* called me to ask about something for a presidential speech. She replied, "Who the hell is Karl Rove?"

Ha! That brought me back to earth. (Karl turned out to be like a brother to me. Now my mom knows who he is.)

That said, sometimes your opportunity to move up comes unexpectedly. It did for me in the summer of 2007.

Early that August, I had flown to Seattle with Peter. He was going to be running in an overnight relay race through the woods (yes, he's a little bit crazy). Our friends Susan and Keri Whitson were going to be there too, and she and I planned to drive to the Oregon coast to meet them when they crossed—or crawled across—the finish line.

On the plane across the country, Peter and I had time to

catch up. There were no distractions—back then, Wi-Fi in the sky wasn't reliable, so I'd put my BlackBerry away and we talked. We'd been open with each other about how my work-life balance was way out of whack. At that time, I was the principal deputy press secretary. Tony Snow, an amazing communicator and lovely human, was the press secretary. He was also being treated for colon cancer, and it had been challenging to manage it all (for him and for me).

Tony was generous with sharing his access to President Bush with me. In fact, he had me attend the early morning senior staff meetings on his behalf and turned to me to handle all of the president's press conference preparation. One of my favorite compliments I ever got from President Bush is that he was never surprised by a question when I'd done his prebrief (that's partly because I was supervigilant, a little lucky, and a lot paranoid—so I covered all the bases with him before he called on the first reporter).

With a year and a half to go until the end of the president's second term, the chief of staff, Josh Bolten, had put the word out to the senior staff that if anyone didn't think they could make it to the end, they should leave soon so that they could have fresh legs into the final lap. He said the president intended to sprint to the finish. I was barely walking to the finish at that point.

So I broached the possibility of leaving the White House with Peter on that flight. He and I wrote up a list of pros and cons. I distinctly remember that one of the pros I wrote down was that if I didn't work at the White House, I'd be able to browse at Target without having to respond to emails. It sounds so silly now, but I remember that feeling. I'm pretty sure, looking back, that I could have browsed at Target and then looked at my emails later. A lot of the time, the pressure was self-imposed. I've learned a lot since then.

Bottom line, by the time we flew back to Washington, D.C., I had decided that I should turn in my resignation. I wasn't going to be moving up to the top job before the end of the administration, and I would be able to get a jump start on a post–White House job (whatever and wherever that was going to be). I had so much FOMO about it—before that was even an abbreviation. My fear of missing out on work I loved for a president I deeply admired and enjoyed being around, not to mention all of my friends at the office who had become like family to me, was so strong. But my love for Peter and my desire to have more time with him had won out. And it sounded so practical.

"I'm getting my wife back, and she's getting her *life* back," Peter said.

I went to the White House that next Monday morning full of angst. Before the communications meeting, Ed Gillespie asked if he could see me at the end. I said, yes, I need to talk to you too.

At the end of the gathering, he said, "Dana, can you stay for a minute."

I thought my heart would gallop out of my chest.

As the last person left the room and shut the door behind them, I was about to blurt out my news when he said, "Do you mind if I go first?"

"Sure," I said. I sat back.

"The president would like to name you White House press secretary on Friday," he said.

"He does?" I asked, immediately knowing that my life

had just changed dramatically, in the short and the long term. "But what about Tony?"

Ed explained that Tony was going to step down and focus on his health and his family. The news was a secret until the president announced it at the end of the week.

This came as a tremendous shock. I can still feel the reverberations from it.

"What do I need to help get it announced?" I asked, jumping in to get started.

As I walked down the stairs of the West Wing to the press secretary's offices, I knew my first call would be to Peter. I shut my door, sat down at my desk, and dialed up Peter.

"How did it go?" he asked, knowing how hard it was going to be for me to resign.

"Peter, they're naming me the press secretary on Friday," I said.

God bless him, Peter said, "Congratulations, my darling! This is wonderful!"

There went his wife. And my life changed dramatically.

At the press briefing on Friday, the reporters were shocked when President Bush entered the room. He gave Tony a lovely tribute, and then he asked me to step up with them.

He said that Dana Perino is my new press secretary. He smiled at me. I blushed. I kind of wanted to shrink back—I liked being behind the scenes better than I craved the spotlight.

Then he said something that I'll never forget.

"And I chose her because I know she can handle you all," he said.

That was such an empowering moment. He was simultaneously letting the press know that I had his full confidence and that when I spoke they could be sure that I was speaking from a position of knowledge and strength.

It also told me that I was chosen not just because I was next in line, but because he thought I was the best person for the job in that moment.

I keep a photograph of that announcement in my home, and one in my office of the president kissing me on my forehead as we said goodbye to each other on January 20, 2009, when he and First Lady Laura Bush went back to Texas. The bookends of that year and a half hold me together even still.

In the days between the press secretary announcement and his last day at the White House, Tony Snow was my biggest supporter. He gave me such encouragement.

I'll never forget how on his last day, he came into my office.

"How are you doing?" he asked.

"Well, not very good. How am I supposed to replace you?" I said.

"Stand up. Come here," he said. I did.

He put his hands on my shoulders and made me make eye contact.

"You're better at this than you think you are." He gave me a little shake.

I didn't feel that was true at the time. But a couple of weeks later, I was rushing to get to the press briefing on time (I never started late; sign of weakness), and I didn't have my notes with me. I hesitated at the threshold to the Brady Press Briefing Room. I decided to just step forward without my folder. I walked up to the podium, said I had no announcements to begin with, and called on Terry Hunt, the most senior wire reporter in the room.

I ended up having my best briefing to date that day.

It wasn't until later that afternoon as I was walking from one meeting to another that I realized something. That's what Tony had meant. That I didn't have to be like *him*. I could be like *me*.

What a concept!

I will always be grateful to President George W. Bush and the late Tony Snow—and all the people who helped me do one of the most impossible jobs in government and communications. Without them, I wouldn't be writing to you now.

So, for you, what's that next big step that would change your life?

And what is your key differentiator that will make you the indispensable choice for the position?

I believe mine has been that I am a voracious reader. And I always try to be the most well-read person in the room—especially the White House briefing room. Knowledge is indeed power. The more I read, the more powerful I feel.

But it never ends.

I still wake up every day thinking I know less than the day before. This has served me well. I jump in every morning to scour the news. It's a bit of a desperate-yet-controlled race to read enough to keep my head above water.

Today I supplement my reading with podcasts that help me gather information. This has provided me some flexibility to get things done around the apartment while I learn what the news is and what smart people think about it. I also use the "listen" feature of the *Wall Street Journal*. The robot reads me the editorials while I make the bed. She's a good companion.

For you, your key differentiator might be your ability to keep up with the latest technology. Or maybe you're good at handling difficult customers or landing new business by closing a sale. You may have "big sky" strategic vision or you're proficient in handling all the details. Or you might be a terrific writer, able to get a new grant approved that keeps your organization afloat.

Whatever it is, press your advantage. Keep honing those skills and be the person they can't do without. Then also work on your weaker skills. I live by the motto "ABL"— Always Be Learning.

That's the surest way to go from a midcareer job to the position of your dreams.

DAN BARR

What are the key qualities of people who succeed at the top levels of an organization?

I have come across very few successful executives or leaders who weren't very smart. One CEO told me that "smarts" is like speed in sports—very hard to teach and it covers for other shortcomings. "Smarts" is multifaceted. There is the more traditional definition: the ability to analyze and process complex information, draw inferences, recommend solutions, make sound judgments and adjust when necessary. Street smarts are also critical. If book intelligence isn't informed by real-life practicality, it is of limited use. And the concept of emotional smarts or intelligence is also very important. The genuine desire and ability to listen to people and the willingness to ensure the success of others is so important. I frequently come out of meetings with very high-powered CEOs saying, "What a smart, nice, practical, and down-to-earth person." There are a lot of really smart people out there, but the ones who have those other qualities and an overarching sense of right and wrong separate themselves from the pack. They are the ones who create followership.

PHIL LAGO

What qualities do you believe make a great leader, especially in high-pressure situations? How do you handle stress and maintain composure when faced with difficult decisions or crises?

COMMUNICATE!

Effective communication is a two-way street; it involves both transmitting and receiving. Concentrate on the message you want people to hear, rather than the message you're trying to send. There is a big difference. Use a collegial and collaborative approach to get your audience to share with you what they heard. Recalibrate as needed. Be clear and transparent. Don't get this wrong.

Effective leadership is not only about leading during times of prosperity, but also leading through periods of crisis. A good leader understands the need to provide clear direction and strategies during difficult times. Ask for and listen to input of others. Remember, if leadership is constantly in crisis, modem indicate that the crisis is the leader.

PAUL MAURO

What sort of management tips can you provide to people who are going from employee to manager? I imagine that it was different on the police force as you moved up the ranks to have people report to you. What approach or skill worked the best in your opinion?

Management is a tricky gig, and it's different from leadership. So ask yourself first: Do you want to be someone who just keeps the enterprise rolling, while playing it safe for your next move in the organization (i.e., a "manager")? Or do you want to break new ground, and lead people there?

Most of us will say the latter but eventually default to the former. It's easy to be beaten down by circumstances and bureaucracy.

The trick for me was always to keep my own management/leadership guidance simple. There are all sorts of curricula out there on management, but I'd say to pick a few basic principles that make sense to you, and stick to them. Bear them in mind when you're challenged or confused, and they'll generally get you through.

For me, those were 1) praise publicly, criticize privately; 2) consider who you would like to be led by, then try to be that person; and 3) don't tell people what to do—tell them where you want to go, and let them surprise you by their ingenuity.

The first two I learned from the NYPD. The last is a version of a quote from General George Patton.

If you've ever had a supervisor who you respected—who you didn't always love, but whose judgment and consistency you admired—I bet that whatever principles you decide on, that person had them. So as you formulate your guiding principles, ask yourself: "What made that person effective?"

And remember: once you're only "managing" and not leading, it's probably time to move on. For your people's sake and for your own.

LAUREN FRITTS

You are not afraid of technology. The next frontier is AI and you're jumping in. What is the best way to stay sharp in ever-changing tech skills?

I fundamentally believe that the experience of trying new things outweighs the fear of not knowing. I don't need to be an expert, but I'm always up for challenging my mind.

My career has thrived alongside the rapid evolution of technology, compelling me to experiment and adapt. I view technology as a catalyst for efficiency and creativity, driving my work forward. I skip the instructions and tutorials and resist the immediate urge to reject something that could potentially change our way of life. Instead I jump into new technologies, embrace change, and eagerly anticipate how they can bring my ideas to life.

Here are some tips from my experience with new apps/technology:

1. **Dive In:** Embrace with a hands-on approach. Experimenting with new tools and platforms allows me to quickly grasp how to use them effectively. This practical approach fosters rapid learning and sparks creativity.

2. **Learn from Others:** Check out what others are doing and see if you can re-create . . . watching what they

do, asking questions, and leveraging their knowledge. People, especially with something new, are often eager to share information and it will help you learn it quicker.

3. **Apply It to Your Job:** Integrate new technologies/apps into my projects. By putting theory into practice, I solidify my understanding and showcase my adaptability and innovation.

DAN BARR

Do you have a sense for how people should be dealing with the coming AI revolution?

The coming AI revolution should be embraced. Every profession will likely be impacted in one way or another. Those who do not embrace it will likely be unprepared and left behind for the upcoming changes and disruptions to workflow. We are in the early innings of the AI revolution and it is moving at a rapid pace. Companies are embracing and leveraging the power of AI to deploy and monitor systems and workflow with minimum manual effort. Companies will gain a strategic advantage with increased innovation, efficiency, and speed due to this technology.

It would be wise for professionals, especially those early in their careers, to familiarize themselves with technology such as ChatGPT, CoPilot, and Gemini with the caveat that this technology is not 100 percent accurate and a work in progress (e.g., Google's Gemini controversy). If you are well versed in the functionality and deployment of AI, your knowledge will result in potential career advancement.

Organizations have deployed AI technology to assist with recruitment, data aggregation, employee engagement, talent development, training, workforce planning, and communications. AI technology such as Eightfold, Paradox, and Modern Hire have been adopted and are currently being used by many organizations.

PAUL MAURO

You work hard to keep up-to-date with new technologies and have a particular expertise in cybercrime. How do you advise people to stay current as the technologies are changing so quickly, especially with artificial intelligence?

This is both easier than ever—and tougher. Easier because there are so many newsfeeds, apps, and websites that you can use—often for free—to stay apprised of developing technologies.

But tougher because things are changing so fast. It is no exaggeration to say that AI is going to change our lives like nothing we've seen since the internet. It's already starting.

It's easy to get blinded by all the information coming down. My own approach is to pick a few venues that I have found to be valuable—in my case, newsfeeds that arrive in my inbox—and stick to those. If they're any good, they'll keep you apprised of at least the main developments. They'll also be a resource to delve deeper if/when you have to.

A last point: ensure you are digitally organized. Notes you make, outlines you want to save, reading you want to catch up on—ensure it's all easily retrievable. There is no force multiplier like organization. And this is doable with all the apps out there. I hate to admit it, but without my phone,

I feel diminished. I left it in an Uber recently and was surprised at how panicky I felt.

We're all cyborgs now. Might as well lean in to it.

GREG GUTFELD

What is an undervalued skill people need to learn along the way?

Do not underestimate the powers of persuasion. I know so many people who are intrinsically right but will never persuade anyone because they're more interested in being right than being able to change a person's mind.

Sometimes being right needs to be relegated to the back seat in order to become persuasive—it's a long game versus the short game. Therefore in a debate or a conversation, to cede a few points here and there, but not your central case, you will almost always be more persuasive than if you were to demand that someone accept every point you make as gospel.

When we see people who demand to be right loudly, it actually hurts our points that we try to make. It's also beneficial to learn to like being wrong—to treat it as though it's just new information that improves your persuasive abilities. Do not be married to a position so much so that you would go down with this ship because then you appear ideological as opposed to arguing on good faith.

DAN BARR

What are the qualities or skills or accomplishments that HR managers look for when considering significant promotions?

Here are my thoughts. I have broken my answers into two categories: experiential and leadership.

Experiential

Companies known for having best-in-class management-development systems are great at proactively ensuring that high-potential candidates check specific critical experiential boxes. They achieve this by having individuals progress through thoughtful, meaningful job rotations.

Since every industry, company, and corporate function (Finance, HR, IT, PR, legal, etc.) is different, the requisite experiential skill sets will vary somewhat. I think young people should make it a point to understand what these prerequisites are so they don't look up one day and realize that they have a lopsided resume with multiple boxes left unchecked. In the best companies, C-suite executives will be able to rattle off the experiential "have to haves" so aspiring "hi-pos" should make a point of knowing them. Everyone needs to own their own career.

For example, during my seven years at Pepsi, I rotated through six different jobs in six cities. This wasn't a case of musical chairs. . . . To the contrary . . . each move had been thought through and approved by executives responsible for grooming the next generation of leaders. They were tasked with ensuring that up-and-coming talent gained experiential exposure to the things the company felt was important.

I think my own experience as an aspiring human resources professional will be illustrative and can be applied to any number of other aspiring executives in other fields. Pepsi felt it was important for HR executives to get exposed to working with unionized (Los Angeles and New Jersey) and nonunion (Phoenix and Pueblo, Colorado) workforces. I worked in field-based (plant/factory) environments where I learned the business (how do we make money) and my function (HR) by observation and hands-on ownership (doing). I then rotated to corporate headquarters, which allowed me to do deep-dive rotations in specialized areas of HR such as leadership development/training, compensation/benefits, labor relations or recruitment, etc.

In these assignments one learned from subject-matter experts and gained proficiency that would be needed if I went on to run HR somewhere someday. Armed with this functional depth, I went back out to larger field roles where I had to manage and lead people. These roles also facilitated exposure to senior executives and allowed them to check me out. Since PepsiCo is a global company, it was imperative to do an international assignment... preferably an "in-country" assignment. Pepsi sent Paula and me to London for a couple of years in order to check that box.

Of course, not all companies are as good at this as Pepsi was. It isn't uncommon in such places to see a young person hitch their wagon to a "godfather" or "godmother" type who would simply bring that person along with them. There are advantages to this but it can and usually does result in an incoherent set of experiences and a resume that makes no sense.

So, those are my thoughts on the experiential side. Then there is the leadership framework. These also vary some-what by industry or company or function, but I have tried to list the ones I think are common in simple terms.

Leadership

1. **Set the Agenda:** ability to diagnose the problem, prioritize, think things through, adjust as directed

2. **Drive the Agenda:** adopt an execution mindset with a bias for action; gain buy-in from your team and bring people along with you

3. **Do It the Right Way:** espouse values, integrity, courage, unselfishness, and support the success of others

Some of these are skill/knowledge based and therefore teachable. Others are more inherent to the individual and very difficult to change and ultimately become career derailers.

JOHNNY JOEY JONES

What do you believe are the top three qualities that make a good leader? What will be your leadership legacy?

The best leaders don't make perfect decisions, but they make good ones. Consistency is probably the single most important thing a leader can espouse. It takes commitment and discipline to be consistent. You have to set priorities and fundamental beliefs, show them outwardly, and consistently ascribe to them and abide by them. If you're going to come up with an idea or policy that's good for the team, but asks more of the individual, you can't start getting lazy on it at the first sign of adversity. Hard work is most effective when it's relentlessly consistent.

My dad always said, "Don't just bust the rust, polish the chrome too," when referring to cleaning his truck from the undercarriage to the roof every Wednesday and Sunday of my adolescence. I think he meant it literally, but he showed it in his leadership as well. He spent plenty of time showing me what I could do better, but he also spent as much time pointing out what I did well. He understood the value in positive feedback. Taking the time to invest in someone and what they do well is equally as important as showing them what they're doing wrong. The goal of a leader is to build a whole greater than the sum of its parts and you can't do that with criticism alone.

Lastly, a leader creates a mission that transcends the task. A task-oriented person will get told "find me a flight to Houston on Sunday" and stop the moment no plane tickets are available. But a mission-oriented person will come back with a Greyhound bus ticket, a plan to fly on Saturday, a rental car on hold, and an offer to drive themselves. When you get your team to believe in the collective mission, the task is simply a means to the end, and your team sees the bigger picture and is invested in it.

JESSICA TARLOV

Many people wonder about the benefits of pursuing an advanced degree after graduating from college. You pursued more education after obtaining your four-year degree. What should people consider when making this decision? And do you recommend working in a job before going to graduate school—or just plowing ahead?

There are no magic carpets to getting where you want to go professionally. Throughout graduate school, I thought there was no way I wouldn't get the offers I wanted because I had all these fancy degrees. Who would say no to an LSE PhD? Turns out, plenty of people.

I've found that advanced degrees—outside of if you want to be something like a lawyer or a doctor and absolutely need the graduate education—are becoming more of a nice intellectual accessory than a must-have in the job market. It's a compelling addition to your resume, but there are lots of folks who have more relevant work experience for the role and become the more appealing candidate as a result.

A graduate degree also doesn't impress like it used to. Employers are much more discerning about the *type* of degree you've gotten and what skills you may have gleaned from doing it. The cost is outweighing the benefit for many people.

All that said, I wouldn't trade my experience and know that now that I've been working for over a decade, my graduate degrees are helping me along more than ever, in researching skills and knowledge. But I do wish that I had worked beforehand to get some hands-on experience to help me focus on exactly what I want to pursue or at least have something on my resume besides being in school to help get a job.

In the end, I'd say to pursue a graduate course more out of a desire for intellectual growth, rather than out of a desire to become a great candidate for a job. There are other ways to get a job.

DAN BARR

Are there key skills that people starting out can develop if they want to move into management?

There are specific training programs that all good companies will offer to new managers. These tend to be skill/practices-based and can be very instructive. I tend to focus on things that should be at a person's core. Things that say more about what they are like as people rather than tactical skills like how to run an effective meeting or how to provide feedback, etc.

So, I think all aspiring managers need to ensure that they have an *informed* moral code. They need to be willing to stand on principle. This has always been important, but especially so in these crazy woke times. If you know who you are, you are less likely to bend to pressure or regret your actions. People will respect this and will be drawn to it.

Also, people aren't going to give themselves over to someone who isn't committed to their personal success or well-being. So, I would treat everyone with great respect. Get to know what makes them tick and try to be of help to them, even if it falls outside of your area. The best leaders create followership because they have moral authority and their teammates know they care for them and their success.

GREG GUTFELD

How did you learn to become a good manager when you moved into an editing role?

I was terrified when I was made editor of *Men's Health*. Although I was their editorial creative director, I really never had previously had anyone "under" me. The best piece of advice came from one of my late mentors, Denis Boyles, who said "you gotta leave behind your coworkers; no more drinking with them."

I assumed he meant that for me—that I would have to be "seen" as a boss now. But it was for the employees. They *need* to see you differently, and they need time apart from you, to be able to vent about you and your irritating habits and mercurial behavior. It's mutually beneficial, because you also save money on bar tabs. But you end up spending time alone, which is maybe the hardest thing for a while, at being a boss. This advice hit home when the British *Office* TV show appeared, and I was editing Stuff magazine, carousing with my staff. I saw the main character, David Brent, desperately needing to be liked. He wanted to be seen as cool among his workers; he wanted to drink with them and so on—and he appeared pathetic and insecure. Once I saw that, I realized you can never fall into that position. No one respects you, and they actually start to dislike you.

The mistake new bosses make is the desire to be well liked. It's important to be friendly and helpful, and identify good workers and reward them. But it's also to weed out the bad. You can't let personal feelings intervene, so stay away. Your job is to lead, not to entertain. Creating a great product and allowing employees to excel and feel rewarded in their own work is all you should be doing.

Chapter 4: Dana's Takeaways

- Listening is a valuable skill for managers. Listen with intent and avoid interrupting others.

- Commit to being up-to-date with new technologies. Staying a step ahead can give you a competitive edge.

- Work on your skills of persuasion. This will help you keep a team motivated and ensure better results.

- Drive the agenda. Take the lead—don't wait to be led.

CHAPTER 5

Keep All the Plates Spinning

(Work-Life Balance, Stagnation, Burnout)

The most frequently asked question during mentoring sessions—and one of the hardest to answer—is "How do you maintain a healthy work-life balance?"

First, that's funny, because I don't think I have a healthy balance (more on that below).

Second, it's so hard to respond because there's no objective answer to this question. Balance is completely subjective—my idea of balance might be your idea of hell or of wasting time when I could be working (or partying!).

Third, I truly believe that everyone has become too obsessed with this issue and it's causing unnecessary anxiety. This is coming from someone who used to hide in the bathroom on the third floor of our Capitol Hill rowhouse responding to emails during the White House years so that Peter wouldn't get frustrated with me working all the time.

So, I realize I'm not the best person to ask about this.

I do respect the worry and concern about work overtaking your life, though.

Let me see if I can give you some perspective on how you can change your thinking about work-life balance, offer some tips that work for me that help me find decent equanimity, and make you feel better about where you are now and how you can feel better about how you spend your time.

To begin, you should realize that everyone I know struggles with balancing work and home life. Whether you are single, a busy parent, or retired with lots of activities on your plate, time goes by so fast. It's astonishing.

Recently, someone asked me if I was bummed that it was Monday already. I said, heck no. Blink and it'll be Friday.

Time goes faster when you're older. Finding ways to pack in all you have and want to do gets more difficult. Prioritizing is critical to a happy life.

The truth is, everyone is just trying to make it. Yes, some people seem to have all their stuff together, everything figured out. But . . . it's never true.

One of my mentees is recently married and wants to have children soon. She has a pretty intense job in the tech industry. She asked me for some time, so I had her meet me for a pedicure. A girl must be efficient!

My mentee said that she looks at a colleague of mine—a mother of two young children who has a lot of responsibility at work as she climbs up the executive track—and thinks she's got it all figured out. That she's perfectly balancing everything she has to do at work with raising her children.

I laughed out loud and nearly messed up my new polish. "Do you have *any* idea how many times a week she and I get together to talk about how to handle all the pressures of wanting to be everything to all people all at once?"

My colleague doesn't have it all figured out. Neither do I.

But there are things I do to help keep some sanity. Here are some tips I've picked up along the way:

- Pick out your outfit the night before to save time and agony in the morning. (Thanks, Mom!)

- Set aside time for prayer, meditation, silence. (I always have ten minutes in the morning before getting out of bed. Then I add in a guided meditation at some point during the day to reset before *The Five*.)

- Accept invitations to only one evening event during the workweek. (This is great advice from the CEO of Fox News. It means making tough choices and missing out on some things, but it's a healthy way to get through the week.)

- Set some boundaries at work for when you'll be available after normal working hours. (For example, if you need to put your kids to bed by 8:30 p.m., let your colleagues or employees know that you can't respond until after 9. You'll be pleasantly surprised how many people will respect this. And if you're a late-night emailer, schedule your emails with tasks to be sent out in the morning. Work karma works!)

- Don't explain why you're not available. (A friend told me her mom gave her this advice—that no one is entitled to know why you can't accept an invitation. Stop providing the reasons you're not able to make it. This was very difficult for me, because I want people to understand why I decline their invitation. But once I started saying, "Thank you for the invitation. I am unavailable that evening." Then I say nothing more and hit send. Overexplaining is unnecessary, can backfire, and sounds whiny about my workload or like I'm bragging that I have something better to do. Simplifying my responses has been helpful to me.)

- Exercise in the morning. (This is difficult to do especially if you're trying to get a healthy amount of sleep; however, if a meeting is added to your schedule or something else happens that prevents you from getting your exercise in, most people will delete that from their schedule because everything else is important for work or family. I find that even twenty minutes of a Spin class, strength training, Pilates, or yoga in the morning really helps get the day off on the right foot. Then I try to fit in more exercise during the day. But if I always do something in the morning, I've at least crossed one thing off my list before work starts.)

- Dedicate time on a calendar. (To protect your time, put it in the calendar. I do this for my Pilates and ballroom dancing sessions. That way if someone wants me to go to a meeting or do an interview, I can work around that time or, on occasion, reschedule my lessons. But people get to know that you're un-available on Thursdays at 2:30 p.m. and they start to work around that. It also helps you mentally prepare for a busy week if you can look at the calendar and see some time blocked off just for you.)

- Prepay for events to make sure you go. (If I cancel my Pilates within twenty-four hours, I still have to pay the full price. This makes me really think if it's worth it to cancel—often it isn't. When you've paid for a lesson or an experience, like a Broadway play or concert, or even a package of massage sessions, you're more likely to keep that appointment.)

- Set limits on social media apps. (I'm guilty of mind-less scrolling on the internet, which wastes a lot of time and leads to many unnecessary purchases. Once I learned that I can set limits on how many minutes a day I'm on Instagram, I relaxed instead of reaching for it every time I had a free second. This is a good way to get some white space back into your calendar and some quiet time for your mind.)

- Outsource where you can. (This is something that's not always easy to do because you either feel like you should be able to do something yourself or the cost of hiring someone to do something for you is too high. However, if you do a cost/benefit analysis of the time you'll need to spend on something like organizing your closets, unpacking after a move, or planning a party, you might realize that finding people to help you do those things will save you something you care more about—your time.

- Take your vacation days, and be mindful of colleagues to make sure it all works out for everyone. That way you can unplug and not have to worry about being away. Plus, if you're a manager, you should absolutely be able to be away from your office and have everything run seamlessly in your absence. (This was one of President Bush's rules for his staff. Once I said I was going to cancel my ten-year anniversary trip because of the financial crisis. He said, "Do you not have a team that can handle things when you're away?" Yes, sir, I do. "Then you go. We'll be fine. Trust in them and yourself." He gave the best advice.)

- Use the rule of three. When you're asked to do something that isn't a part of your regular work, ask yourself: Is this something I want to do? Will I make money doing it? Will it help a cause I care about? (Sometimes the answer to one of those things—it will help a cause you care about—is all it takes to get to yes. Sometimes even making more money won't make it worth it. But if you feel overwhelmed with requests, this is a good way to streamline your thinking. I first heard this advice from talk radio host and Fox News contributor Leslie Marshall about ten years ago. It has served me so well and I pass on her advice to a lot of people struggling to keep all the plates spinning.)

Balance is made easier by exercising good habits—nutritious food, healthy sleep, decent amount of movement and exercise, and a spiritual connection—something that reminds you of the bigger picture that keeps you both grounded and in awe of the world, whatever that may look like to you.

Plus, socializing in some way—book clubs, dinner with friends, parties where you show up for others, group fitness—keeps you connected with other people. We are social animals, and being a part of the world can help you feel more balanced and happier.

And when you feel like you're failing, it's okay to fake it till you make it. Sometimes just acting like you've got it all under control can lead to it being true.

Balance is in the eye of the beholder. And it evolves over time. What you're looking for in your life will change from your twenties to when you get married or make partner at the firm to when you're ready for a new challenge or to slow down a bit.

The hope is that you find work you enjoy with people you like to be with, and that together you produce a good product or service. And that you have family and friends who enhance your life when you're not at the office.

There are some wonderful suggestions that follow about how to balance your career and your life.

I'd like you to remember this as you read through this chapter: Work—and life—and the work-life balance is what *you* make it. It is up to you to make good choices, to stay true to your principles, and to raise your hand when you need help. If you commit to doing those things, you'll be able to land on what works best for you and your family.

And just when you have it all set, life will throw you another curve ball. You'll be in better shape to handle whatever else comes your way.

Because there will always be something else.

And that's part of the fun!

DIERKS BENTLEY

Time management seems to be a common challenge for many of us. Being a working parent is hard enough, but being a working parent and a country music star who is constantly on tour must be very hard to juggle. What is the hardest part about leaving your kids behind when you hit the road? How do you maximize your productivity and make the most of your time each day?

Lately I've been trying to do less! After so many years of trying to be multiple places at once, I'm trying to pull back a bit and do less, and do it better.

I love the road, but I hate being away from my family—that definitely is the hardest part and is the reason why I got into aviation. I realized once our first kid came along that I really needed to find a way to cut the corners off my travel. I started flying a single-engine four-seat piston plane in 2009, which allowed me to stick around for an extra night at home and morning, instead of being on the bus, and enabled me to fly home sometimes right after the show ended. I've had a sponsorship with Cessna since 2015 and am type-rated to fly a Citation jet. Not only has this been life-changing for me, but also for my band, who fly with me whenever I do. When I am home, I do every school pickup and drop-off that I can and just try to be as present as possible in all the daily-life stuff. For our family, going on a walk or hike at a nearby park whenever schedules allow is our best and easiest way to reconnect.

But I would say I have my best days when I get seven hours of sleep and do some sort of workout early in the morning before school drop-off. I find I am way more productive if those two things are accomplished.

MARTHA MACCALLUM

As a national news anchor, you juggle a demanding career with the equally significant role of being a devoted mother to your three adult children. What do you find most fulfilling and rewarding about parenthood? What is your best advice to new parents?

Your kids always come first but it is also important for them to understand that you take your work seriously. Children learn everything by your actions; they grew up watching my husband and I work hard. We both love our work, but when we got home, we played with them, read to them in their beds at night, and when they were older, we went to their games, and took the day off to be there for special things. But we also traveled for work, were away sometimes, and missed some things.

But now I see that they are diligent and professional in their own early-stage careers and I think they turned out pretty okay. Also, we prayed with them every night and tried to show them how much they need God, and how much he loves them. Now we have so much fun with our young adult kids, we treasure them, they still need us, and they are still figuring things out—but man are they fun to hang out with!

BRET BAIER

Your son, Paul, was born with heart problems and has undergone multiple open-heart surgeries and angioplasties. That must be tough to watch as a parent. What have you learned about yourself throughout that whole process? How has this experience shaped your understanding of resilience and personal strength?

Everybody has something—this was our something. Paul was born with five congenital heart defects and his first surgery was at ten days old. He's had five open-heart surgeries and ten angioplasties to fix his heart. And now—he's six foot three and very happy and healthy. I learned that prayer helps in dark times, that thinking about positive outcomes and how they will feel seems to get you to the light at the other side of the tunnel. And I learned that you always have to be your loved one's advocate. Paul is the resilient one and because of that resilience we have learned how important every day is. In the hospital, we always said we were "one day closer to going home." Now we're home and he's healthy and we try to cherish every day.

MICHELE CHASE

You run a very successful business, and a very busy household. I can't imagine juggling your email inbox with morning car pool, plus your kids' football, wrestling, and soccer, much less carve out any Michele time. But you do, because I see you socially (so fun!) and you paint beautiful pieces. How do you prioritize self-care and maintain boundaries between your professional and personal life?

It was difficult to decide to keep working when I had my third son. It was a pivotal moment of being overwhelmed. I had a new promotion, and now a new baby coming. It was really hard to believe that I was going to be able to continue working. It was *a lot*. I look back at how it was hard when they were little, but amazing at the same time. My boys have seen me working, know that I travel for work, and we're very well adjusted to that. They also know I always return home with some little gift from someplace.

Continuing to work, and working where I had the support of my boss and colleagues, I continued to progress in my career to accomplish something I never thought was possible for myself.

I certainly don't do it alone. My husband is helpful and very much involved in everything we do as a family. I also have help. We have always had wonderful sitters who make sure the kids are shuttled from place to place. I've also had supportive workplaces where my CEOs have ensured that I had some flexibility to attend to the kids when I needed to.

There really are three things that keep me sane having a busy life at home and at work.

1. First is something my mom told me when I had kids and was working: leave things in a "comfortable state of undoneness." Nothing will ever be completely done. There's always something that you can't quite finish completely each day. You do as much as you can to know where you have to pick up tomorrow . . . that could be at home or at work. Life is messy and you need to give yourself the grace to NOT be perfect. You get done what is important to get done.

2. Second is compartmentalization. I very much compartmentalize my life when I'm at work and when

I'm at home. When I'm at work I get deep into what I'm doing. I don't get distracted. And when I'm home and with my kids and family, I compartmentalize to my family time to make it quality time with them. Of course, the two worlds bleed into each other at times. If I have something I need to remember for my family, I'll put reminders in my calendar to allot time for it so I don't go through the whole day and forget it. Even when I travel for work, you can get so busy with coworkers and talking that I will put a reminder in my calendar, so I remember to call the kids before they go to bed. Same thing for the weekends when I know I have something that needs to be worked on . . . I schedule it so I make sure that I made space for it. Maybe it sounds crazy but it's so easy to forget things or just miss your window of time that was needed for that one more thing.

3. Lastly, when it comes to my self-care, I have "me" time by waking up at 5 a.m. just to go to the gym or ride my Peloton. Nobody is awake and even my dogs sleep in since I don't feed them at that time. I grab a cup of coffee (yes, I brew it the night before) and I do something just for myself to start the morning, which puts the whole day in the right order. Then I can focus on everyone else. The other thing I do is, when I'm feeling overwhelmed, I'll go into my little studio (it's nothing fancy, just a little space in the storage area of my basement) and I paint with music on and either a glass of wine or a cup of tea.

ELISE BITTER

New moms need some self-care too! What's your advice for them when they feel like they barely have a moment to breathe? With your son Brady about to turn two, what's your reflection on being a mom and a professional? What's been the most rewarding part of juggling both?

It can help to discover your resources prior to having the baby, such as meeting with a lactation consultant to learn about breastfeeding or pumping. Learn to be okay with letting someone else that you trust take care of the baby. Ask for help from a spouse, parent, friend, babysitter.

You are not a bad mom if you need to take a walk, get a pedicure or massage, or simply take a shower. If you don't take time for yourself, then it'll be hard to show up enthusiastically for your child and you will feel depleted. If you are struggling, don't be afraid to reach out to a therapist or a psychiatrist for some additional support.

For as long as I can remember, I have wanted to have kids. At the same time, I've worked my whole life and career to be where I am today as a business owner of my New York City–based private psychotherapy practice. The most rewarding part of both is that I care deeply about my identity as a mother and as a therapist. I love my child and my work, and those can coexist.

It was pretty incredible to me that every single one of my clients returned to working with me even after my maternity leave. I joke that my career has given me some experience as a mother, as I care deeply about my clients' success (as if they were my children), the same way I do for my child's well-being.

AINSLEY EARHARDT

How did becoming a parent change your outlook on work-life balance? Any tips for young people thinking about having children and how they can manage both?

I have the best of both worlds. I have a full-time job in a career I love—working a morning show from 6 a.m. to 9 a.m. eastern. I technically can be home with my child all day, during the day. When my daughter was a baby, this schedule worked perfectly. I would go to work while she was sleeping and then have the rest of the day with her. I had a full-time job but also took my child to all of her music classes, ballet classes, read to her, and played with her all day. Then she began preschool and I became very involved in her school as a volunteer during the day and was able to stay active in her daily life.

I am grateful that my job is complete (for the most part) before her day has really begun. I always wanted to be in New York City and working in television in some form. I wasn't ever sure if I wanted to be a mother, but then . . . in my midthirties, I changed my mind. I wanted a baby badly. I struggled to get pregnant for about a year, then had a miscarriage and finally had my healthy daughter. At this point I begged God for a child. I desperately wanted to be a parent. I was in a place financially where I could afford a baby in Manhattan (I would need a larger apartment and a private school tuition) and could spend more time with a child given my morning show schedule.

It all worked out and being a mother (I am a single mother) filled a void in my life. She is my world and we spend every day together. If you have the desire to be a mother—do it. It's the best decision you will ever make. Life is very busy and you don't get as much sleep as you would like, but for me it works well and we figure it out one day at a time. I don't have the work-life-mom balance completely figured out, but I have support from friends and loved ones and seem to manage both.

MORA NEILSON

You run a very successful business, and a very busy household. I can't imagine juggling your email inbox with morning car pool with your three kids, much less carving out any Mora time. How do you prioritize self-care and maintain boundaries between your professional and personal life?

Laugh. Laugh at how utterly insane, complex, complicated, full, and intense our lives are and thinking we can do it all. Look at your life and the trials and tribulations with a humorous lens—it truly brings a sense of levity to it all. If your life was a movie (and not a drama flick but a comedy) you would give yourself much more grace and understanding for what you are trying to do and accomplish. I'll bet you any amount of money seeing your life as a comedy will leave you happier, more content, and void of guilt and shame.

SALENA ZITO

Time management seems to be a common challenge for many of us. Despite trying various methods like setting earlier alarms and multitasking, I often find myself feeling like there aren't enough hours in the day. How do you maximize your productivity and make the most of your time each day?

I hold one full-time job as the national political reporter for the *Washington Examiner* as well as a contributor for the *Wall Street Journal* and *Pittsburgh Post Gazette,* and I am syndicated in scores of small and large newspapers across the country. Which means I am often doing at least seven or more stories a week that require travel, detailed on-the-ground reporting, plus often talking to officials either elected to office or running for office.

If I looked at my day like that in the morning I would never get out of bed—it would be that overwhelming and intimidating.

Whether I am working from home or on the road, I take a brisk walk first thing in the morning. I really like getting up at 5:30 and doing that. I often take a pencil and notepad with me and list what I must accomplish that day while I take my walk (another way to do that is just send yourself a note using voice-to-text but I really like the act of writing).

I will usually have a story or two leftover from the day before, and that is the key thing: you need to bank interviews from the day before so you have slept on them and can take them on in the morning; then set a goal of writing one story by 10 a.m.

Take another walk around the block.

Then get on the phone and spend the next hour and check in with sources across the country to see what is going on in their communities; phone calls are really important. I cannot stress that enough. Even if you don't get a story that day, you have established communication, you interact, and you get a sense of what may be coming.

If I am home I drive a mile to my daughter's house and play with the grandkids for an hour, you cannot imagine how soul-invigorating that is.

PHIL LAGO

How do you approach self-care and stress management, especially during busy or challenging periods? What advice would you give to someone struggling to make healthy lifestyle choices while juggling a demanding career?

Manage the crisis; don't let it manage you. Use tools such as whiteboarding and red-teaming to better explore your options. Understand that your data has an expiration date.

Make time to refresh and relax, whether that means working out, meditating, or engaging in another activity to help you decompress. Don't forget your family and don't forget everyone else has a family.

BRET BAIER

What strategies have you found most effective in consistently setting and reaching your goals?

I find I am constantly using visualization to imagine what achieving my goal or goals looks like and what it feels like when I get there. I guess it's basically my version of "the Secret"—and always starting from a place where you are grateful for what you have. Finding out what your goals are and setting them is the most important part. Write them down.

ANDREA ARAGON

Looking back, what are your best tips for moms working to manage work and family?

Being a mom is hard. Being a mom who works outside of

the home is even tougher. I was fortunate to have the support of my mother and husband, who played a daily role in trying to manage the wonderful chaos of children, professional commitments, and our sanity. There were many moments where I felt tremendous guilt when I was home thinking about work, and conversely, when I was at work thinking about home. If possible, ask for flexibility at work so you can be present for those important moments. You will never regret the time you took to be there for your family. Now that I am a fairly new empty nester, I often (but not always) miss the craziness of parenthood. It does go really fast.

MICHELE CHASE

How did becoming a mom change your perspective on life?

I think before the kids, work was my job, and my job was me, if that makes sense. My identity and life were just centered around that. When I had kids, it didn't make me less engaged or less invested. It was just different. There were more things to care about, and work just didn't "feel" like it was the everything.

I think having kids gave me perspective on what to care about and what not to care about. If work was feeling too heavy or even aggravating at times or there were politics in the office, I just didn't care enough to get involved in the nonsense that might have been happening. I remember a certain executive who was super-high-pressure and pushing all the time. I was so excited when he was having his first child because he was going to have something else to put his focus and energy on.

And it gave him perspective. I think it made him a better

leader. You can still have high expectations for yourself and those you work for as a parent, but it gave me—and my one hard-charging friend—a little more grace not only for ourselves but also for others.

TOM SHILLUE

In your book, Mean Dads for a Better America, *you reflect on your childhood, growing up as one of five kids in a devout Irish Catholic family in a small town outside Boston. What values from your upbringing have influenced your life as a father, and how have they shaped your parenting style today?*

Mean Dads was aspirational for me because the tough love we got from our parents was the norm growing up in my hometown, and I've always wanted to model my parenting after that. My wife and I say, "If only we could be as mean as our parents were!" It's a little bit tongue-in-cheek, but it's real too. We want to resist the safe-spaces and "everyone-gets-a-trophy" mentality and give our kids the benefit of the rough-and-tumble childhood that we had.

At the opening of the book I tell a story about my mom pushing me out the door on the first day of kindergarten.

"Where do I go?" I asked her.

"Just follow the other kids!" she said. "You'll get there!"

There wasn't a lot of handholding, and children were expected to learn from siblings and friends. But it wasn't just because the parents were tough—there was a practical element to it. People had big families and didn't have time for the kind of helicopter parenting that you see today.

Remember the Boy Scouts' motto, "Be Prepared"? When I wrote the book I realized all my stories were like little lessons

I had learned, so I made each chapter a different distinct value, with a merit badge to go with it: "Be Tough," "Be Resilient," and "Be Bold."

The first chapter was "Be Afraid," in which I compare my dad to Darth Vader from *Star Wars*. Was he really that scary? No. But a little fear can be good for you.

From *Mean Dads for a Better America*:

I spent much of my childhood in fear. Fear of God, fear of my parents, fear of the other adults in the neighborhood, fear of bullying kids. But fear is not always a bad thing—it keeps you alive. Fearing actual danger is very important. As you grow up you learn which fears are real and which are not, and it's always liberating to discover when one of your fears is unfounded. You think, my dad is going to kill me when he finds out! But then he doesn't kill you. You live to see another day. Your dad is not a murderer—that's great news to a kid!

MARTHA MACCALLUM

You once shared some advice with a young woman and colleague of ours who was feeling overwhelmed managing her job and raising young children—that you would only allow yourself to look three months ahead. How did you land on that approach and how did it help you?

Yes! I've never been much for the "where do you picture yourself in five years" interview question. I eagerly took each challenge as it came and did what made me satisfied and happy. With my young children and my husband and I both working long hours, we took it sometimes an hour at a time! But especially heading back to work after my maternity leaves, it was always hard to put that suit on and go back. My heart would break just thinking about it with a new baby in my arms.

But at the time, my mom said, just try it for a few months and don't think too far beyond that. When I looked at it that way, it seemed manageable, and little by little we figured it out.

I think my kids have benefited also from the experiences and work they've watched me be part of in my career. They've even had the chance to tag along—for national political conventions and to Normandy for the seventy-fifth anniversary of the landing. Now they are grown, and I give them the same advice when they look to me, not sure which road to take with their careers or opportunities. I give them the same advice Mom gave me: If you're feeling the pull or even a twinge of excitement, try it and see where it takes you. You can always change your mind if it turns out to be the wrong way. Twenty years later, I'm glad I chanced it!

CHARLES PAYNE

How do you approach the balance between investing and saving for the future versus enjoying the present?

For me, they are the same thing. Often, people tell me they feel sorry for me for working so much and at that very moment, I feel sorry for them (they do not love what they do). Each day I learn, each day I engage in the world, and each day I try to help people. I have other interests I'd like to pursue, including philanthropy, travel, and drawing. From time to time my crew comes over to watch sports or work on cars and I see my children often.

ELISE BITTER

With the rise of remote work, some individuals find it challenging to create boundaries between their personal and professional lives. What tips do you have for keeping a healthy work-life balance while working at home?

The most important thing you can do is to communicate your boundaries ahead of time by agreeing on a time that you will not be on your phone or at your computer.

If a colleague doesn't respect that and messages you at 2 a.m., resist the urge to reply until your typical office hours. If you reply immediately, then you're playing into the pattern, signaling that it's okay to be contacted at any hour of the night and you'll be expected to respond immediately in the future. Don't let that happen.

For remote Zoom calls, I recommend spending some time on making sure your setup is comfortable and looks professional. Think about your backdrop. Your unmade bed is a no-no, but maybe a nice plant and a cute photo of your dog could work.

Also, make sure to use a good set of headphones for calls and turn on a sound machine to prevent your work colleagues from hearing your partner whipping up a protein shake in the kitchen. But have a good signal so that if you want a shake too, one will appear at your desk without skipping a beat.

SALENA ZITO

What habits or practices have you found helpful for maintaining a healthy work-life balance and avoiding burnout?

It is pretty simple. A walk around the block—sometimes five blocks depending on the story or the day always clears my mind and helps me shake any anxiety I have over meeting deadlines or getting the story just where I believe it should be. It does not matter if I am home or on the road. I will find a way to either walk around my neighborhood, or find the closest park or trail when out of town, and just get out rain, shine, or snow (just not ice) and walk the anxiety or pressure off. The fresh air is remarkably good for your psyche; the change of scenery often helps to see a story more clearly and often inspires, and it is good for your heart.

LYDIA HU

You are a wonderful mama to two beautiful kids. If you could give one piece of advice to new parents, what would it be?

When I first became a mom, I wanted my daughter to have every experience from the start. Baby massage class? Sign us up! Swim class for infants? Definitely! Prayer circle at church? We would never miss it!

I thought I was expanding my baby's horizons; what I did not realize is that I was building a new community of support. I met fun, interesting, smart people who were also embarking on a parenting journey. These are people I would turn to in moments of need. I asked for pediatrician recommendations and advice on how to manage sleep regression.

Sometimes I simply needed someone who understood what it is like to push through a day of work when a teething baby meant you got no sleep the night before.

My advice is to seek out these groups. Build and nurture the relationships. These people will become a new community with whom you will share some of life's most precious moments and help you get through the more trying ones.

Don't worry about making a mess. A mess can always be cleaned up. Worry about missing the fun.

SANDRA SMITH

How do you navigate the challenges of being a working mom while striving for the elusive work-life balance? Can you share any strategies you have found helpful for being fully present in your children's lives and excelling in your career at the same time?

I actually think it is harder on me than it is on them. I remind myself often: everything will be okay. The goal every day is to give 100 percent wherever I am. If I am working, I am completely focused on that. If I am parenting, I am completely focused on that. My biggest challenge is managing everyone's schedules. A very organized, color-coded calendar is a must! If it's not on the calendar, it won't get done. I also like to embrace the simple things like packing a lunch or bringing my kids' favorite Popsicles to the game. Remember to enjoy these sweet moments!

JIMMY FAILLA

Dad time! Tell me about a moment that your son taught you something big about life? Also, if you could give one piece of advice to new parents, what would it be?

I have one kid, mainly because the state would never let us have two. I'm not saying I'm the worst parent in the world but when I was three months into homeschooling Lincoln during the pandemic, he randomly asked me during Spanish class, "What date do we celebrate Cinco De Mayo on?" I wish I was kidding, for his sake and mine.

But the thing I learned early on is that having a kid is actually great for someone with big ambition because it teaches you a level of efficiency that you will rarely attain unless you are in the upper echelon of self-starters.

You see, the thing is, when you're single, your free time is your own and you can do whatever you want with it, which can lead to stunning levels of procrastination. I tried to write jokes about this in my twenties but I never got around to finishing them. But once that kid comes, those fleeting moments of free time are when you *have to* get things done. So it quickly transforms you from a guy who spends ten hours on the couch watching kung fu movies to an actual ninja who can conquer the world in the forty-eight minutes you have before he starts crying for a bottle.

The best advice to young parents is to teach your kids to have fun. Because being able to laugh in life is the greatest survival skill they'll need, and the good news is you don't need money to do it. When my son was born, we were so poor my wife had to make cloth diapers from scratch. But Lincoln had no idea because we were always too busy laughing to notice the financial shortcomings. Seriously. Plenty of people have driven their kid to school in a jalopy. I once dropped my kid off in a yellow cab.

The sad part is, I was so broke, I had to charge him.

But we laughed every mile of the way. So don't worry about the rat race, or keeping up with the Joneses, because you can have more fun than them in any tax bracket. And if we're being honest, the odds are the Joneses are gonna get divorced anyway.

JEANINE PIRRO

You raised children as a working mom. Is there anything you wish you had known then that you know now? And what is the best advice you pass on to new moms?

It was not easy being a more-than-full-time working mom, often on trial while my children were young. I wish I recognized that the job would always be there, but those special moments with your children would be fleeting.

Motherhood does not change your focus, your drive, or your ambition. It simply adds a new dimension to your life experience in ways that benefit you, expand your horizons, and for many women, complete you.

LYDIA HU

Do you have any tips for new moms who are nervous about returning to work after maternity leave?

Budget time to test your childcare routine before your first day back at work. For example, start daycare a few days early so you can practice the drop-off and pickup schedule. This will help work out any surprises (like a longer-than-expected line at drop-off!) before you have the added expectation of being at work on time. And maybe you can treat yourself while someone else has the baby!

JOHN ROBERTS

Your twins—Sage Ann and Kellan Clay—are absolutely adorable. If you could give one piece of parenting advice to new parents, what would it be?

I give this piece of advice to them every day: "Be a kid, but take everything that you do seriously." My father, who was only around for five years of my life before he passed, liked to say that "any job worth doing is worth doing right." For the most part, children are averse to hard work. And they don't realize how hard you have to work at something to get good at it. Allow children to explore and determine their own passions. But when they find them, encourage them to work hard.

One other piece of advice: Keep them off devices until they are at least thirteen. Teach them the value of conversation. I see two-year-olds on devices at restaurants. That's just building a lifelong addiction.

It's a tough battle, but one that can potentially save years of distraction and declining interest in outside pursuits.

ANDREA ARAGON

What you thought you wanted to be when you grew up changed as you got older. Is the same true for your now-adult sons? And how has your experience and career journey helped you guide your children?

Finding your passion is key to establishing a satisfying path in life. My husband and I have tried our best to help our sons establish a solid foundation of discipline, responsibility, and accountability. They know how to look people in the eye, shake a hand, and listen with respect. These skills, along with a strong work ethic, pave the way for incredible opportunities.

My eldest son, Freddie, is just completing his first year of medical school. After several injuries in high school sports and the death of my beloved aunt from cancer, he knew unequivocally that he wanted to become a doctor.

My youngest son, Evan, is in his junior year of college and is still exploring what he wants to do. That is okay. You do not always have to have the answers. Just be open to different opportunities and be ready and willing when these opportunities come calling.

JESSICA TARLOV

Did you get any advice that was really helpful when you first became a mom? And once you had Cleo and decided to have another baby, what was your thinking about finding and maintaining some semblance of a work-life balance?

There is so much good advice out there for expectant/new moms. Take it all in and see what applies best as you go through this totally crazy and amazing journey. Tidbits from others that have resonated with me include taking help when people offer (seriously, do this!), give yourself grace (especially when it comes to your body, which has spent nine months growing a person and then going through a major trauma to get them out), and sleep when you can (no explanation needed).

But the advice that was most helpful, and that I admittedly struggled to embrace, is that a baby doesn't need much else besides you. This isn't about pushing a breastfeeding agenda (I didn't breastfeed either of my daughters), but more about understanding that even if you feel like you're failing or your child is going through a phase and pushing you away, you're still their everything. You know them better than anyone else. You love them more than anyone else.

You get them. And they get you. It always comes back to that.

As for the decision to have a second baby, my husband and I knew that we would be happy as a family of three if that's what was in the cards for us, but that having a sibling, especially as you age, is such a value-add. We were lucky and it was easy for us to have Teddy, but the anxiety around setbacks to my career was raging. Especially doing this in the midst of an election year!

Two things helped:

1. Having a supportive employer. I know that's easier said than done, but it's a hard road to be a working mom and be somewhere that isn't geared toward making sure parents get ample time with their newborns and recognizes that family comes first. Something to think about!

2. Having a great support system. This is bigger than your partner, if you have one. It's about your whole ecosystem, including friends, family, colleagues, and neighborhood. Your life changes in ways you didn't even imagine possible, and you need everyone to be on board with that.

LAUREN FRITTS

You are a creative person, an artist with many talents. How does having a hobby take you out of work mode and does it also help make you better at your work? When you were so busy and constrained from an artistic outlet, what happened to your work output, mental state, and creativity? How would you advise people to make time for an outside-of-work activity—be it art, sports, reading for fun, or dancing?

Everyone needs an escape, a passion that lets their mind breathe. For me, it's painting. When I pick up a brush it's like a meditation. I think about nothing else but what is in front of me. Interestingly, the busier and more stressed I am at work, the more vibrant and imaginative my art becomes.

It's like when you played too much Nintendo as a kid and had to blow into the cartridge to make it work again. Am I dating myself? Well, that's how our brains work too. When you're overthinking or overworking, engaging in something you love acts like a magical reset button, enabling you to return to your tasks with a sharper focus. If it worked for *Duck Hunt*, it can definitely work for your next big project.

So pick a passion, whether it's painting, pottery, dancing, reading a good book, or playing soccer or tennis. Carve out time in your calendar, commit to it, and watch how much brighter and more balanced your life becomes.

BRET BAIER

Beyond your role in the anchor chair, you're known as a dedicated golfer with a deep passion for the sport. What lessons have you learned from your experiences on the course that have positively impacted other areas of your life, such as your work ethic and overall perspective? Why do you believe it's so important for individuals to find meaningful hobbies outside of their professional pursuits?

Golf is a metaphor for life. Some days everything is going right and then you hit a tough patch—you hit one out of bounds or three-putt from twenty feet. Golf teaches you to play one hole at a time and never give up. You never know when you'll go on a tear and birdie a number of holes in a row, despite a rough patch in the middle of your card. Hobbies take your mind to different places and give your brain time to "breathe" away from a daily grind. Golf is my escape.

DR. MARK SHRIME

You also competed in American Ninja Warrior—*that's a remarkable achievement in itself. How did having that commitment actually help you with work-life balance?*

When it comes to work-life balance, I'm not necessarily sure I'm the world's best example! Surgery and *Ninja Warrior* both select for people who go all in!

What *Ninja* did give me was different. Yes, it was a hobby, one that I adored, and in that way it gave me something outside of work to spend time on. But more than that: it gave me a community and it taught me what to do with fear.

Bring any group of people together trying to tackle what feels impossible, and you'll necessarily forge lifelong friendships. When I started, *Ninja* was still in its infancy. So we were a bit of a ragtag group trying to push the limits of what we were told our bodies could do. That forces you into a vulnerability with yourself and with your training partners that spills over into your nontraining life.

And also: pushing the limits is terrifying. You could get hurt. You could fail. You could do it publicly, in front of cameras and family and spectators. *Ninja* taught me that bravery wasn't standing up on the starting platform without fear. It taught me that the fear was never going away, and that I had the choice to let it make my decisions for me, or to decide for myself.

STEVE DOOCY

Your cookbooks have been incredibly successful. What motivated you to turn your hobby into published books?

My wonderful wife, Kathy, suggested we write a cookbook. And her pitch was simple: "Everybody eats three meals a day, and everybody wants to make sure that meal is tasty." She was right, and it led to us writing the Happy Cookbook series of three books, which wound up as number one *New York Times* bestselling cookbooks.

The premise was we all have foods from our childhoods or histories that remind us of happy times. For me that happy food was my mother JoAnne's pot roast. A simple recipe with a chuck roast stewed for hours under a slurry of cream of mushroom and dry Lipton onion soup mix. When I was growing up, I could not imagine any food that tasted any better, anywhere. I still adore it. When Kathy makes it on my birthday (as my mom did), when I walk into the house after it's been cooking all day, that aroma takes me back to our little house on the south side of Russell, Kansas, when life was simple, my parents were alive, and we were all together.

Shortly after that cookbook was published, I started getting email and messages from people who would say, "Steve, I made your mom's pot roast—loved it."

In the years since that recipe was published, I have heard from hundreds, maybe thousands of people all around the world with the same basic message: *Steve, your mom's pot roast is terrific. We make it all the time.*

I love that right now somewhere in America somebody is making my mom's roast.

Ironically, her advice to me and my sisters was "Share the good things in life."

She had no idea she would share so much with so many people she would never meet in her lifetime.

What a great tribute to my mom.

JESSE WATTERS

Your mom says that the most important thing you can teach children is to be resilient. How has that helped you as you're now a dad of four and managing a lot to raise your family and win in prime time?

My mother is a child psychologist who does assessments of children's learning abilities and in the course of her research has found that the trait of resiliency is the key factor in determining a child's success at the time and later in life. My father always stressed hard work while I was growing up. Sunday chores, manual labor, the hot summer sun, and preparing extensively for tests. Grit is your ability to push through external challenges, or even internal, maintain a steady focus, and get the job done at a high level over and over and over again. Raising a family, hosting two shows, and writing books creates pressure and time constraints. Having the ability to initiate action, complete tasks, and manage your time every single day of the week year after year while business and life throws curveballs can be distracting and tough, but if you enjoy the work and are committed to an unrelenting pursuit of growth, the resilience exists at all times and becomes a part of you.

TYRUS

Staying healthy—for you it has been important for your livelihood—you had to be fit and healthy in order to wrestle and act. Now it's also incredibly important, because you're the head of the house, and people are relying on you. What do you want people to know about the importance of being the healthiest they can be?

The biggest thing is listening to my body, not my ego, and that's hard for me. I'm an alpha male to a fault. I identify with Boxer the horse from *Animal Farm*—he worked and he worked until he gave out. He split a hoof. And it sent him to the glue factory. But even then he still only wanted to work harder. I strangely envied Boxer as a young man and wanted to have that work ethic.

Now as an older man I realize how having a strong work ethic is great. Like Boxer, I never want to complain or ask others to help. But you have to pay attention to your health and can't throw that away. A man's mentality—my mind frame—is I'm fine, I'm all right. But you have to listen to your body and hear it when it says to take a rest.

Knowing when to take the weekend off or spend time with my family, that's smart and wise and I have to work hard still to put myself in a position to take that time off. This is still a struggle for me.

But if you ask me how I'm doing or feeling? It's always the same answer: "maintaining," which is my cool word for I'm all right.

JOHNNY JOEY JONES

When I asked you about being a girl-dad, you told me, "My daughter breaks my heart with a single tear and welds it back stronger with a single kiss. As a man, I grew up learning that my purpose is to provide, protect, and love. Having a daughter amplifies those core tenets by a million." What is your best piece of advice to give to new parents?

My best advice is to acknowledge the privilege you have to be the parents of this amazing life you're responsible for. From that comes a purity and clarity to drive all other emotions and actions. We have a responsibility to teach and guide our children as they become who they'll be for the rest of their lives. That doesn't mean simply incorporating them into our lives, but more so being present in theirs. Asking questions about their day, providing explanations to why they can or can't do something. Being consistent in our discipline and love, equally. Prioritizing our time "with" them, not just the time we spend "for" them such as work or driving them to practice. Being present might be the hardest ask, but it's also the value investment we can give them.

BENJAMIN HALL

You've talked about being out of balance with work and family. How have you worked to improve on that front. Any tips for the rest of us?

For some years I believed that working constantly and building a career was the best thing for my children's futures, and so I would work and travel as much as I could in order to provide and build for them. It meant I was never home for dinners, was abroad often, and I missed school plays and sports days, etc.

But I got that wrong. I should have been firmer about the events I needed to be at, and not miss them, and known that they were more important than an assignment, a show, or an opportunity.

That being said, it is very hard when you're building a career because you do have to make sacrifices, and if you don't do it, someone else will. So I don't hold it against anyone who has to focus on work because that is often the reality of the world we live in. But find a balance, set aside times and days to be with them, and just don't miss those.

I now know that my children would be leaving home, and I would have missed so much of their childhood without noticing. Today I have found that balance, and make sure I'm at everything I can. I see it in their eyes too.

Chapter 5: Dana's Takeaways

- No one has the perfect work-life balance. Just keep trying to find yours.
- Movement and exercise are key to a clear head and healthy existence.
- Eating well can help you better handle long hours and stressful periods of time.
- Work smarter, not harder. Get your routine down in the evenings so that you can have better mornings.
- Find a hobby. Schedule time to do it. Take lessons to get better. And don't be afraid to play a game or enter a competition. This helps with work-life balance.

CHAPTER 6

What Matters
in the End?

"Why are we here?" I've often asked myself. Meaning we, as humans, on this earth. What in the world is this experience we're all having? What's the purpose, the point, the significance of life?

These thoughts are profound and come to me at random times—doing a routine chore, driving down a road, or preparing to go live on election night.

These are strange moments that can stop me in my tracks. It's almost like the feeling of déjà vu, but even more disorienting.

"Why are we here?" is a big, open question. It humbles me. Fills me with wonder. And it's in these moments that I feel close to God.

"I guess this is all up to you, isn't it?" I ask Him. "Yep," He says as it all carries on.

Good deal. You're in charge, sir.

As I wrote in *And the Good News Is . . .* and *Everything Will Be*

Okay, I need to be reminded over and over that what I'm planning doesn't matter. I can't script my life—and increasingly, as I get older, I realize I don't want to. I am learning to like not knowing what's next. God's in charge of that, and it's a good thing—he's sure to do a better job than I would.

So, while I don't worry as much about what is going to happen next, I very much want to know what *matters*. It's so easy to get caught up in trivial things. And it's remarkable how we must learn life's main lessons repeatedly.

Even as an adult you have to be reminded that:

- comparing yourself to others is a sure way to feel miserable; don't get hung up on what others are doing;

- worry is a waste of time and should be converted into energy that calms you or propels you forward;

- being wrapped up about what other people are thinking about you is a waste of time—they're too busy thinking about themselves;

- what you do and how you act when no one is watching is a measure of your character—and being proud of who you are is key to finding serenity;

- the people you surround yourself with can determine your level of happiness and your success;

- helping others is the best way to feel connected to this life, and it's the surest way to help you answer, "Why are we here?"

In writing this book, I've realized that we're all really pulling to get to this point of what *actually* matters. And when you reorient your thinking this way, a lot of the worries about trivial issues go away.

Consider psychologist Abraham Maslow's hierarchy of needs when it comes to our lives. Here's my take on how to approach it from a work-life perspective:

- **Bottom line:** work puts food on the table and a roof above our heads

- **Security:** saving and investing enough money to be able to manage an emergency (being laid off, a health scare, an accident)

- **Relationships:** committing to another person to build a life and family, and having enough good friends to share the ups and downs with

- **Fulfillment:** achieving your career goals, being confident in your work, having meaningful relationships that share in this success

- **The point:** having gratitude for a significant life well lived in the service of others

My colleague the former congressman Trey Gowdy wrote in *Start, Stay, or Leave* that we should reframe the way we think about what matters most in life. He said that instead of defining what success looks like to us, we should think about what we consider significant.

I liked this framing because it gets more to the heart of what we're doing here. Many people will achieve success—they'll graduate with honors, win an athletic competition, rise to the top of the corporate ladder, start a business and sell it for a million dollars, serve at the highest levels of government, and more.

But if they aren't doing something with that success, something that *matters* to them, then success ends up feeling hollow.

And to me, significance is something you can apply to every part of your life:

- Are you making a difference in your neighborhood?

- Can you be present with friends and listen to them without thinking about your to-do list or worrying about checking your phone?

- Have you found someone to commit to, someone to share life's journeys?

- Is there a cause you care about that you've contributed to in a meaningful way?

This reminds me of Lawrence Jones, a young man from Texas who grew up wanting to go into law enforcement or the military but ended up being a great journalist covering those issues and more. You will hear more from Lawrence later on in this book.

Three years ago, Lawrence volunteered to raise a service dog from Baden K9, an organization devoted to helping U.S.

veterans with post-traumatic stress disorder (PTSD). Lawrence wanted to bolster their mission by using his platform to provide awareness about the importance of military dogs and what they mean to their handlers and to our safety. It's been a huge responsibility, and he wears it lightly and happily upon his shoulders. He didn't wait until he was at the end of his career to have a significant impact on the organization.

Lawrence has provided a great example of doing what matters to him as he's climbing up his career ladder. Plus, Nala is definitely a good conversation starter. She's quite the wingwoman!

In today's workforce, a lot of young people are looking for their employers to represent values they care about—but this is a minefield for companies whose main responsibility is providing a good or service at the best price that will allow them to pay their employees and grow. Almost all companies don't exist to comment on today's politics and culture. Obviously, some companies have been snakebit by this (see Bud Light, for example).

It isn't up to your employer to be helping you feel that you're making a significant difference in the world. That's up to you. And you can do it well. In fact, separating the two is beneficial to you and to your employer.

I remember former secretary of state Condoleezza Rice telling me a story about how she was counseling some young college students who said they want their first jobs to be meaningful. She responded, "Here's what will be meaningful. You'll go to work and do a good job. Two weeks later, you'll get a paycheck. *That* will be meaningful."

Then as you grow older, get more experience, and build

up your ability to donate time or money to causes you care about, that will be meaningful too.

I've found that mentoring younger people is a great way for me to make my career have greater significance. Forget the titles—the experiences that I can rely upon to help someone get through the next big stage of their lives are invaluable.

They're . . . significant.

And so maybe that's what we're supposed to be doing with our lives.

We do our best, with good intentions, integrity, and authenticity, until one day way in the future we get that answer to what in the world we were doing here.

DIERKS BENTLEY

You are a multi-Grammy-nominated artist and one of the most humble guys I know. In a recent interview, you mentioned that your children serve as a "great equalizer," keeping you grounded and down-to-earth. Could you expand on the significance of humility in your life and career?

To make it as a country singer, songwriter, or performer, you have to spend a lot of time listening to and studying those who came before you. I think for me, having such an appreciation of the history of this music and city, I had no choice but to be humble! I'm such a fan of not just the big stars everyone knows, but the songwriters and musicians and legendary people who have worked in the business. I think that keeps you humble.

And when you've had some success and start feeling

pretty special, there's nothing like your kids to help remind you that you're not! I love the story Keith Urban told me one time about being on the road when his girls were young. He was getting ready to walk off the bus and head to stage and said to his daughters, "All right, who's ready to go watch Dad rock the house?" And the girls replied that they would prefer to stay on the bus and finish watching whatever Disney movie they were watching! My kids have kept me humble like that many, many times.

LAWRENCE JONES

You shared with me one of the best pieces of advice your mom ever gave you: "Having a little case of nerves is always okay. It shows you have a little humility. When you stop having those nerves— well, you're just full of yourself." How has embracing this advice supported you during your first few months as a Fox & Friends *co-anchor as well as during other pivotal stages of your career growth?*

I equate the nerves I feel doing TV to the nerves I had before tip-off in my basketball games. You need a little of that—arrogance will cause you to make stupid mistakes.

No one knows everything but being in the news business . . . there's this unspoken pressure that our audience expects us to know everything. We don't (especially for someone young as me).

Our audience does expect accuracy and humility. I've learned to go in every day expecting to make some but not the same mistakes. The moment those nerves disappear is when you will make fatal mistakes. The nerves are the result of a conviction of wanting to get it right!

JIMMY FAILLA

You are one of the most energetic and optimistic people I've ever met. What's your secret to living life to the fullest?

The story I always tell is that I'm like "a dog with a job." Do you know how, when you go to the airport, the dog that sniffs everyone's bags is always excited and his tail is wagging at a billion miles an hour because he can't believe they're counting on *him* to save the plane?

That's me. Every time I walk onto a TV set or a radio studio, I can't believe they're counting on me to save the show.

So my advice is to remain humble enough to realize you started off in a place where you were wildly unqualified to do the high-level work you're now doing. But in being blessed with such an incredible opportunity, the only way to show your appreciation to the universe is to do the hell out of your job and be a force multiplier of positive energy wherever you go.

MARTHA MACCALLUM

What role do you believe mentorship plays in career development, and how can individuals find and cultivate meaningful mentorship relationships?

Honestly, one thing I think I missed out on a bit was building those relationships at work when I was younger. I had work buddies, but I was always rushing home to the kids when work was done. Now I truly enjoy helping to nurture some of the young talent we have at Fox. The great thing about getting older is that you really have learned a few things. I love passing them on, encouraging their work ethic, and watching them hit it out of the park.

BRET BAIER

You've often cited Brit Hume as being one of your greatest mentors in your career. What to you makes a good role model? And how can individuals find and cultivate meaningful mentorship relationships?

A good role model is someone who exemplifies what you're looking to emulate in one way or another and someone who you look up to. For me, Brit has been my mentor and friend since I came to Fox twenty-seven years ago. Because of the grace he showed me, showing me the ropes early on, I feel compelled to do the same when I can. Mentors can be crucial in career development. To find a mentor, search for someone you look up to and take the chance to reach out. In most cases, that person will bend over backwards to help. They usually did the same thing at the beginning of their career. You just have to take the chance and act.

SALENA ZITO

Can you share a time when you received valuable mentorship or guidance from someone in your professional network? And how did it impact your career trajectory?

The best mentor I ever had was a former editor of mine, Sandy Tolliver. When I started at the Pittsburgh newspaper years ago she was the city desk editor. She had worked her way up from police reporter, who also covered council and authority meetings across the region and had really cut her teeth on the things that mattered most to people: public safety, utility costs, holding local government accountable.

She was, and still is, tough as nails and could smell nonsense from a mile away. She really taught me the importance of skepticism, pressuring an elected official or whoever I was covering to get beyond the first canned answer to the first question.

And she taught me if I had any doubts, to follow that instinct relentlessly. And it is never important to be first with a story; it is only important to be right.

To this day if she sends me a note telling me I've done a good job on a story, I know I've done well. Sandy worked her way up to becoming managing editor in an all-male-leadership newspaper. She did not go to any prestigious college. In fact I am not sure she went to college, which kind of proves that sheepskin does not mean you are going to be the best there is. Sandy remains the best editor and mentor I've ever had.

STEVE DOOCY

Your son, Peter Doocy, decided to follow in his father's footsteps. He joined Fox News Channel in 2009 as a general assignment reporter and has since risen to become senior White House correspondent. What advice did you offer him as he embarked on his career path in news and what has this meant for your relationship?

When I got a big TV correspondent job in Washington, D.C., I had been reporting in Kansas City and had no idea what I should wear to work on TV in the nation's capital, but I remembered the legendary *Washington Post* reporters Woodward and Bernstein from the movie *All the President's Men*. Robert Redford and Dustin Hoffman starred as the two young hard-driving reporters, making phone calls, developing ledes, and hammering out exclusives that exposed the Watergate scandal. They made reporting look important . . . and cool.

You know what I remembered about the movie version of the reporters? They never relaxed. Always working, even when sitting down pounding out exclusives on a bulky manual typewriter—which can work up a sweat. So they did the obvious—they rolled up their shirtsleeves.

And you know what it means when somebody rolls up their sleeves: they're getting down to work hard.

So when I started reporting from D.C., on my first day I took off my necktie and rolled up my sleeves, and I automatically looked like a hardworking correspondent—which I actually was.

On Peter Doocy's first day at Fox News, as we were walking into the newsroom, I told him, "Roll up your sleeves." Being a sassy kid he whispered, "Why?" And then I revealed the secret to my success. "With your sleeves up, people will think you're working *on something*, which is really important when the boss walks by."

Peter hesitated a beat and then rolled up his sleeves as we walked to his desk. He hasn't rolled them down in the years since, unless he's in the Oval Office.

My advice to my son: if you're not actually doing much, at least try to *look* busy.

BRIAN KILMEADE

I was so impressed when I learned that you coordinate quarterly networking lunches for your Fox & Friends *staff. Despite your crazy busy schedule (I still don't know where you find the time in the day to sleep), you find the time to take your young employees out to get to know them and their ambitions and offer your advice and invest in their futures. What legacy or message do you hope to leave for others through your career and personal journey?*

My message is that you can get outplayed, you can get outsmarted, but you can't get outworked. You are 100 percent in control of your effort. Add to that, you must learn from mistakes because hustle is not enough; you must be good enough to be successful. Finally, you must answer the "Why" question: Why do I want that job? That career? It can't be to prove to people who doubted you—that's a motivation, but it can't be the objective. That's the reason I didn't quit.

LAWRENCE JONES

Can you share a time when you received valuable mentorship or guidance from someone in your professional network? How did it impact your career trajectory?

Hannity. I would say Sean's three rules.

1. Remember your mom the preacher and your dad the trucker driver.

2. Be humble.

3. Don't get in trouble with the ladies, lol. Be the Texas gentleman.

I had been on the network for a few years. Sean has this thing that he changes his show up a little every new calendar year (somewhat of a theme change). He invited me into his office for a mentor session. He saw me growing in the industry fast and wanted me to avoid some pitfalls. He gave me the advice above.

But after giving me these three pieces of advice, he offered me a job to be his correspondent. I respectfully said no. My reason: I was a libertarian and he was a strong conservative.

He gave me the best advice that I still hold close to this day: "Just be *you*, LJ."

I know it sounds simple, but it's the one thing I remember when approaching topics. My perspective is shaped by my unique lived experience, so I lean in to that.

ANDREA ARAGON

Has there been a mentor in your life who made a difference in your career and/or life?

I can attribute so much of my professional success to the many mentors I have had. While I would not consider myself exceptionally smart, I have done one thing right: surround myself with people smarter than myself.

I am also coachable. This is a huge talent, if I do say so myself. I highly recommend it. I do not know it all, and never will. But I can listen, and I can learn. This is how having mentors can make a tremendous difference in your professional career.

One of the greatest mentors of my life was a community legend. Ray Aguilera was an unconventional community leader, fundraiser, convener, and philanthropist. I met Ray when I was in college when I volunteered to work on one of his foundation's first fundraisers. Seeing a need, Ray established the Pueblo Hispanic Education Foundation, which was created to provide scholarships for students from low-income backgrounds to attend college. Thanks to his vision, dedication, and bold fundraising abilities, the organization still thrives today and has raised over $4.1 million to help eliminate barriers to education and a better quality of life for deserving students of all ages and ethnicities. I admired Ray's tenacity, authenticity, and selfless love for his community, especially children. He was often rough around the edges, but despite this, Ray made things happen. He was bold and fearless, characteristics I wish I had. He passed two years ago, but his values and words of wisdom live strong in my heart.

PHIL LAGO

How do you approach mentorship, and what do you think makes a good mentor?

A good mentor listens and equips you with the tools and information needed to create your own path to success.

Mentors and role models have taught me both what to do and what not to do. My mistakes in selecting role models, who turned out to be different from my expectations, helped me to understand the importance of integrity, empathy, competency, and inclusiveness in leadership.

TREY GOWDY

Throughout life, you'll encounter a variety of advice from many different people. How does one discern the valuable guidance from the noise? Or rather—how to take the right advice, from the right people (and how to block out everyone else)?

Discernment is a gift but even if you don't have the gift of discernment, do you understand human nature and can you frankly ask yourself whether the person giving advice truly has your best interest in mind?

We all have friends who are well-intentioned but out of their depth in offering advice. I try not to take medical advice from investment bankers.

By the same token, I don't often buy stocks based on what my ophthalmologist recommends.

Does the person offering advice have expertise? Your best interest in mind? A track record of giving good advice? Demonstrate wisdom in her or his own life? I take information from a great number of people, but advice from a select few.

Separate information, data, facts, and experience from advice. Seek all the information you can from reliable sources, but we are lucky if we have five people who will truly give us the advice we most need: the best advice for us, not for them. People are, by nature, selfish. Some of the "advice" we get is really for others and not for ourselves. That is the mark of wisdom, that person who can understand us well enough to tell us what we don't want to hear and do it with credibility.

One test for a good advisor is whether or not she or he is willing to risk your wrath. The world is full of people who will tell us what they think we want to hear. Can you find someone who will tell you what you need to hear and say it in such a way that your defensiveness eventually gives way to resignation and then ultimately gratitude that your friend cared enough about you to be honest?

DIERKS BENTLEY

How do you strike a balance between being ambitious and being content with where you are in your career journey?

I never experienced any contentment until just recently. People used to ask me when I felt like I made it. And my first thought was always, "I've made it?!" I honestly think that playing a sold-out show at Madison Square Garden in 2018 may have been the first time I thought that I could maybe start to allow myself to feel some kind of satisfaction.

And in the years since, I've realized that you can have gratitude for and contentment with your success but still be hungry for more.

The biggest danger I feel like for someone at my stage of their career is to be holding on to it as tightly as you did when you were first starting off. I'm still putting in the work to make sure my live shows are the best they can be, that my next album is better than my last.

But at the same time, I'm so happy for the younger artists who are getting their chance to grab the golden ring. I remember what it feels like to be focused solely on one thing for so long. So I love seeing this next generation that's crushing it right now.

BRET BAIER

What's your measurement of success and how has it changed in your later years versus how you viewed success early on in the workforce?

In the early years, the markers of success were easy to

see—the rungs on the ladder of the TV business. But as you realize your goals and what you want to do, success changes and your definition changes. With time, success is measured more broadly about happiness, family, goals outside work. And that evolution is a good thing.

TREY GOWDY

How do you strike a balance between being ambitious and being content with where you are in your career journey?

You must know yourself and whether your ambitions are reasonable and to what are they rooted? Pride? Selfishness? Genuine belief? You don't want to ever appear ungrateful for chances you are given, so when someone hires you, it is decidedly uncool to start looking for the next job. We have all been talking to someone at a party only to have that person look over your shoulder to see if someone more "important" had come in.

What you should strive to hear is a mixture of "you should have left me years ago but I am so grateful for your loyalty."

Leave wherever you are better than you found it. Keep your integrity, which means keep your word. If you commit to a year, stay a year absent some criminality or abuse. Just because we are ambitious doesn't mean we are correct either. Wanting to do something and being good at that something are two different things. I may aspire to be a nightly TV host, but could I genuinely do the job? I know myself pretty well, so I know the answer, which is why I am so content on Sunday night and Sunday night alone.

Know yourself.

Strive, but don't settle.

Be grateful for what you have and let the people who provided it know.

Stay a second longer than most thought you would but leave a second before they wished you had.

MARTHA MACCALLUM

I've always admired your commitment and ability to stay connected to your faith and embody it in your daily life. Could you share how and why this is important to you and any tips you have to help stay connected to God in this crazy busy world we live in?

Honestly, my faith has really grown as I've gotten older. There really were a lot of years when I'd say a prayer at night and with the kids, and we'd go to church on Sunday, but I wasn't really living it.

The change came when we sent our children to Catholic schools. I grew up in public school and something about seeing a cross hanging over the door in their classrooms really touched me. Seeing it integrated into everything they did was wonderful to me.

Recently we all went to Israel on a pilgrimage, a life-changing experience. Also, I had never really read the Bible all the way through, until I committed to doing *Bible in a Year* podcast with Father Mike Schmitz on the Hallow app. It changed the way I looked at my faith, gave me a deeper understanding to go through the Old and New Testaments with guidance. It's a lifelong process and joy to move closer and strive to really know Christ.

LAWRENCE JONES

What daily habit or routine has improved your well-being the most?

Prayer. Intentional prayer.

TOM SHILLUE

I admire your passion for giving back. Can you tell me a little more about this and why you think it's important to pay it forward?

I honestly don't think about this much and I'm always surprised to hear it. Once when I was nineteen years old, a woman nominated me for some local award for "giving back to the community."

I was surprised and thought, "What's this? I don't volunteer for anything!"

But I had helped her organization by making short videos for her. That's something I enjoy doing, and I was willing to do it for free so I'd learn and get better at it. I didn't think of it as "giving back."

But I think that's the best kind of "service" people can do. Just like the old saying about choosing your career: "Do something you love, and you'll never work a day in your life."

In the same way, you should think about helping others by sharing with them the things you're already good at. You'll love doing it, and they will love you for it. It's a win-win!

FRANCINE LEFRAK

What are you most grateful for in your life? How do you actively practice gratitude in your daily life?

I'm most grateful for my resilience, my wings, my empathy, my husband, my support system (including friends like Dana Perino), my courage, my positivity, my passion, and my perspective.

How do I cultivate gratitude on a daily basis?

1. Acknowledge those around me and make sure they know I see them, I hear them, and I appreciate them.

2. I'm conscious of my language. Positive word power transforms your thinking.

3. I write in my daily journal my "good for me list" to reinforce the good things that happened that day and how I contributed to others.

JOHNNY JOEY JONES

What are you most grateful for in your life? And how do you actively practice gratitude in your daily life?

I'm most grateful for the opportunity to have two beautiful, unique humans call me Dad. I can't think of a greater love, or responsibility. I'm grateful because I can look back and see many scenarios where my kids don't exist, yet all these millions of things aligned at just the right time to allow me this moment with them as their father. I take this responsibility seriously. I remind myself to include them as much as possible in my life, but to also be in their lives. I humble myself to get down and experience life on their level, and then I remind myself to mold and guide them with discipline. Not just in what is expected of them, but in what I show them as an example. All of this is work. So I guess I show my gratitude by working hard to earn my blessing every day.

LAWRENCE JONES

What are you most grateful for in your life? And how do you actively practice gratitude in your daily life?

I'm most grateful for my support system and those who paved the way for me. I show gratitude by not only trying to prepare or search for my replacement but also by pouring back resources into the community that raised me.

FRANCINE LEFRAK

You've made a significant impact, but the journey doesn't end with you. It's about passing the torch. How crucial do you believe it is to pay it forward and empower and support the next generation of professionals or aspiring leaders?

It's very crucial to pass the torch. Talent is everywhere but opportunity isn't. If I can create opportunities for people to express their talent, then I feel like I've made an impact.

ANDREA ARAGON

What are some of the life skills you learned as you led organizations with people who had a lot of different opinions about how to solve a variety of problems with limited resources?

Listen!

What an unappreciated concept in this loud world. It has been said many times before, but we often listen to respond, not to understand.

This skill has served me well. It can be hard to do at times, but you can learn so much. In my professional role as a funder, it is the number one thing I need to be able to do. When you listen, you give great value to the person who's talking to you. It is a great gift you can give someone, because so many of us feel unheard.

Another life skill that I value wholeheartedly is the ability to be fair, balanced, and transparent.

Listening is what this is built on. When you listen, you learn, and as you learn, you become more balanced. When you are balanced, it is so much easier to be transparent. This may sound like common sense, and it is. But common sense is not very common.

FRANCINE LEFRAK

In the midst of life's ups and downs, holding on to perspective is key. This is something I like to call Perspective with a capital P—a quality I so admire about you. In today's fast-paced world, it can be easy to lose sight of the bigger picture. What guidance would you offer to individuals who are struggling to keep things in perspective?

Stay in the present moment and appreciate what is in front of you.

Know your truth.

Get good guidance.

JESSICA TARLOV

Finding a life partner can be daunting and overwhelming. Why should people never give up on finding love?

Finding love isn't a straight road, especially when you're living in a bustling city and trying to get your career on track. I broke up with my boyfriend who I thought I was going to marry (we went engagement ring shopping—I wasn't delusional!) just before I turned thirty-six. As anyone who has seen *Sex & the City* knows, single and thirty-five in New York City is a scary place. You're thinking about kids and worrying about your fertility without the right partner, which pushes you to poor decisions out of fear. And prospective partners know you're not someone looking to take it slow/spend a few years just enjoying each other, thinning out the pack of partners.

I was very lucky to meet my husband in an elevator at about 1 a.m. one random Saturday night. I had been on one of a string of disappointing dates. He was the next-door neighbor who had just moved in. And it turns out, the right neighbor for me. Covid lockdown came a couple of weeks later and we were stuck together.

Four years and two daughters later, we're both very thankful for my arguably poor judgment in going to a stranger's apartment in the middle of the night. So this relationship started with a surprise and perhaps fated meeting that could not have been predicted.

I should also point out that he was an avowed bachelor living in the belief he would never get married. So much for how much you know yourself until you fall in love, and then all bets are off.

That's really why you shouldn't give up on finding love. It sustains you in ways you wouldn't have expected. It's a support system, a sounding board, a defender, and an endorphin boost. It makes life transitions—good and bad—more tolerable and even exciting.

And though I'm not someone who necessarily believes in a higher power, I'm sure that love is put in your life to help you navigate difficult challenges.

For me, my dad was dying when I met my husband and I wouldn't have gotten through that without him. For you, it may be something else. But I know it will be made easier for having big love in your life.

Disclaimer: If you want to be single, there's nothing wrong with that. I know plenty of people who are very happy on their own and also wildly successful. But the above is what has been true for me.

DR. MARK SHRIME

Could you describe how you felt once you were able to marry your skills as a surgeon to helping the patients or Mercy Ships?

At the end of my book *Solving for Why*, I mention the Japanese concept of *ikigai*. This is the idea that the place you're supposed to be is the place where four different things intersect: what you love, what you're good at, what the world needs, and what you can get paid for.

Before I started working in global surgery, I was doing something that I was good at and that I could be paid for. All of a sudden, when I moved to applying those skills to something I loved, and that the world needed, the deep dissatisfaction I was living under disappeared.

That's not because the surgeries are different or anything like that. My day-to-day life in the Mercy Ships hospital is not altogether that different from my day-to-day life in normal practice. It's just that I've filled in the other two *ikigai* intersections.

HAROLD FORD JR.

Public service runs in your veins—how important is contributing to your community, your country, as part of a well-balanced and meaningful life?

As a person of faith, my belief is this: one's chief pursuit in life on earth is to try and leave things better than you found them.

JESSE WATTERS

You spend a significant amount of time helping out organizations you care about—in fact, one of my earliest memories of you being on The Five *was your support of your friend who had ALS. How does making time to support your causes help round out your life experience?*

Early in my career when I didn't have a lot of money, I would donate my time. Sometimes I'll do favors for people involved with charitable organizations like invitations, promotion, or networking assistance. I've been fortunate enough to be successful in my field and there's a duty to give back.

I approach charity by giving organically. I accept invitations that are meaningful and close to my heart or home. I help with friends and community stakeholders when asked. I've been involved with organizations that support the military, law enforcement, hospitals, and educationally disadvantaged children.

The government can't address every single issue. It takes the private sector to lead because we're on the ground and are more efficient and targeted.

It's much better to give than to receive. We all know that deep down.

JEANINE PIRRO

Throughout your life, you've made a mark—in particular, you advocate for victims. How important was it to you to create the first domestic violence unit in the DA's office? And how did that propel you to new opportunities?

My mom made me sensitive to the needs of the underdog. I was raised to be compassionate and understanding. The idea that you could beat a woman with impunity because she was your wife made no sense to me.

My passion for a level playing field for the woman who agreed to love, honor, and obey the man who then chose to stab or brutalize her led me to start one of the first domestic violence units in a prosecutor's office in the nation.

That decision propelled me into the national spotlight because of the ferocity with which I prosecuted these cases.

FRANK SILLER

What is it like to receive so much from giving to others—can you describe what that has done for your own well-being? And would you encourage others who are sad or lonely or scared to find a way to volunteer or give back in a way that will break the cycle of their feelings?

The act of giving has brought me an immense sense of peace and purpose. It has helped me navigate my own grief and transform it into something positive. Witnessing the positive changes we can make in the lives of others reaffirms our connection to humanity and our capacity to heal.

I strongly encourage anyone feeling sad, lonely, or fearful to engage in acts of service. Volunteering can provide a

sense of community, purpose, and perspective that is profoundly healing.

HAROLD FORD JR.

*You have so many friends, from your earliest childhood to new
friends you make every week. What is the key to keeping such a big
circle a part of your world?*

Keep an open mind about people, even people who have
been accused and found to have done wrong. We are all
sinners. I'm blessed to meet and know so many people. My
closest friends are family to me. I call them, tell them I love
them, and run to them when things don't go their way. And
I'm even more blessed that my friends care about me.

JOHNNY JOEY JONES

*Can you share a meaningful experience where someone offered
you support or guidance during a challenging time in your
career?*

I really have a few great examples of this and will try to
keep it short.

First was my dad. He was full of sage wisdom cloaked
in simple terms aimed at a specific task. When complaining
that it rained every time I wanted to work outside and make
a little extra money, he once looked at me and said, "Son,
don't you dare cuss the rain. Cuss its timing." I'll be honest,
that one took me a while to understand, but what an amazing
perspective to have.

Stoicism in a pragmatic practice. At face value he was
reminding me how important the rain was to our lives and

the industry in our area. But at an even deeper level he was reminding me the world doesn't revolve around me. That doing something simply because it benefits me in the moment isn't good if it hurts the family or community I exist in. He gave me my first glimpse at what we call the "30,000-foot view" by simply reminding me to see what felt like a hardship in the moment as the blessing it was.

Secondly, while in EOD (Explosive Ordnance Disposal) school as a Marine I went to a staff sergeant with a problem I had with balancing my Marine Corps duties with my duties as a student. He listened intently, allowed me to finish my dramatic performance of how debilitating this situation was for me, then paused. Finally, he looked at me and said, "If you know what the real problem is, you know the solution to it. Don't come to me with a question, come to me with an answer." Then he walked away.

I pondered his words for a minute and finally realized I was passing the buck. I knew what I wanted, but instead of asking for it, I was asking him to figure it out and suggest it.

The underlying lesson is to have the courage to fix your own problems, try to figure out what you think you need, and then go ask for help doing it, or getting it. You may be wrong but at least you've analyzed the situation and found the confidence to take action, as well as practiced the humility to get help and guidance.

TYRUS

You made a good decision to walk away from a life that could have led you down a bad path. When you think back to that moment, what was it that helped you make the right choice?

I grabbed on to television heroes as a child—whether it was the Incredible Hulk, Conan the Barbarian, the dad on *Good Times*, or anyone who showed high content of character. I truly wanted to be a man of high character who always protected the weak and fought for a better tomorrow. And when I was at a point of taking shortcuts in life, that small voice inside me got louder. Also, I came to understand my father's choices and never saw the bad men in my life as who I wanted to be. These dudes were always looking over their shoulders, sleeping with one eye open, and had a pistol as a best friend. That's not how I wanted to live or be remembered.

FRANK SILLER

After your youngest brother died in the 9/11 attacks, you turned your grief into action with the Tunnel to Towers Foundation. How did you manage the interest and explosive growth of the organization to keep it going? Also, you live your life with such faith and generosity. What are the values that you hold to make life a little sweeter?

After Stephen's death, the desire to honor his heroism and keep his spirit alive was overwhelming. The growth of the Tunnel to Towers Foundation was propelled by the community's support and the universal desire to remember 9/11's heroes. Managing this growth involved focusing on transparent goals, creating impactful programs, and fostering community involvement. The key was channeling the collective grief into action, which resonated with many who wanted to remember the sacrifices made on that day.

The values instilled in me from a young age by my parents, Mae and George Siller—faith, generosity, and a commitment to doing good—are the cornerstones of my life. Embracing these values makes life sweeter by enriching the lives of others. Seeing the impact of acts of kindness and generosity not only brings joy to those on the receiving end but also fulfills a deep, personal need to spread goodness in the world.

PETER MCMAHON

When we met on the plane and fell in love at first sight/flight, how did you get over all of the obstacles in our minds—the distance, the age gap, the previous marriages that didn't work out? Why did you choose to go for it and love again? Did anyone give you any good advice during this time?

It was a strange feeling. Having been married twice and while not bitter, I was still a little raw after the last one. My first marriage was a mistake and would have ended much earlier but for the children. In the second my wife decided to look elsewhere, and I had no choice. I had in fact made the decision I was not going to get married again, and was certainly not looking for any kind of relationship at that time. And then I sat beside someone I would have considered out of my league, and we just talked, and it happened. Falling in love wasn't really a choice.

The distance was an obstacle—but no more so than someone from California meeting someone from the East Coast. The seven-hour flight was no worse than the weekends when I drove five hundred miles to see my children, flying being impractical. So I was able to come to the U.S. to visit Dana regularly, and brought her to the U.K. twice. And we spoke every day by telephone.

The age gap concerned me only because I knew it would

potentially be much more of an issue for Dana. Would I have expected, or even probably wanted to be with, a twenty-five-year-old when I was forty-three? Absolutely not. But Dana was wise beyond her years and extremely smart, so for me it never felt like such a gap.

While I was concerned about how Dana's parents would feel about my being eighteen years older than their daughter, and when I took them to dinner I was expecting a grilling, they were very supportive and said that because she's so sharp and mature Dana needed an older man. (Which was certainly a relief!)

My father, who was happily married to his third wife after being widowed relatively young and then experiencing an unpleasant and costly divorce from wife number two, was encouraging and told me that when you have the opportunity to be happy you should always go after it.

The day before Dana came to live with me in England, he asked if I thought I would end up going to live in the U.S. I answered that I had no idea and that it was still too early to make long-term plans. He responded by telling me that if ever I had that opportunity to do that and didn't because I felt it necessary to be near my elderly father and stepmother, that he would be very upset. "It's your life, you have to go and live it as fully as possible."

JOHNNY JOEY JONES

I asked you what honor meant to you and you said:

"Honor is one of those words we give so much reverence to but rarely dissect why. For me, honor is a decision-making tool: Do I act in a way that honors the expectations, sacrifices, and traditions of what and who I represent? Am I worthy in this act of the associations and privileges I have?"

I loved this response. I think it speaks to something else I like to stress upon in my mentoring, which is the idea of integrity. Can you elaborate on this? How important is it to protect your character and personal integrity?

The Core Values of the Marine Corps are Honor, Courage, Commitment. What's so impactful about these three words is that they are almost exclusively marketed as how you can become a better person through your Marine Corps service. They make you feel like you can "be a man of honor, a courageous warrior, someone who can commit to seeing something through."

But in reality all three of these words, in the context of being a Marine, are synonymous with "sacrifice."

To exercise the courage needed to fulfill a commitment and honor a promise takes looking adversity in the eyes, seeing certain pain or failure, and taking it on anyway. And to make that choice, that's integrity. That's putting your most selfish desires aside to be the one who does the difficult thing, not for yourself or your legacy, but for the positive impact it will have on others' lives.

We say "integrity is doing the right thing even when no one is looking." But I think integrity is even simpler than that. Integrity is a genuine desire to seek out the right thing to begin with. We're all going to fail, make mistakes, lie, and let people down. We're human and we have basic primal urges to satisfy our wants and needs. But as some point we learn right and wrong. We learn to respect the effect our decisions have on others and we learn to discern the difference between an easy path for us and a better outcome for all. Integrity is putting this in action and taking that first, difficult step on the path that's better for others, in any situation.

My dad told me before I left to go to boot camp, "Son, I don't care if your job is cleaning toilets, those better be the cleanest darn toilets you've ever seen. Because after you leave, that's all that's left of you and your work. Even if no one knows you did it, they know someone worked hard here."

That's integrity. Doing the right thing void of any positive impact or recognition for you.

Chapter 6: Dana's Takeaways

- Comparing yourself to others leads to negative thinking. Cut out this habit.

- Pass the torch. Give others opportunities. There's reward in approaching work this way.

- Always pass on a compliment.

- A curious mind is an important quality for careers and relationships. Ask others about themselves. Focus outside yourself; that's where you'll find more happiness. This is key to your own happiness.

CHAPTER 7

And Now for Our Next Act . . .

A few years ago, my friend retired after a very successful career in finance. He had been with the same bank for several decades, through many economic cycles: booms and busts, bubbles and bursts, terrorist attacks, the Great Recession, hiring freezes, layoffs, and huge amounts of growth.

Retirement didn't come easy to him. He wrestled with the right time to step down. Finally, convinced that he'd accomplished what he could and looking forward to more time with his wife and family, he called it a day.

At his retirement party, he was overwhelmed by what he heard. Many of the people who worked for him stepped up to give speeches. All of them were grateful for his leadership. Some he didn't know well spoke about how much he had helped along the way.

My friend was revered and beloved. He left a lasting, wonderful mark on the company and the people he worked with. He's not an emotional man, but a tear or two was wiped away by him and everyone in the room.

His story got me thinking. Instead of wondering what people will say at your funeral—which is a fine exercise and something to think about—what about imagining what they'll say at your retirement party? Will you have left a lasting impression (a good one, hopefully)? Helped someone through a difficult time, given them a chance to shine, stayed late to help them finish a project? Been the indispensable leader they needed?

People don't forget those things and they don't always express gratitude in the moment. Wouldn't you like to be able to hear about your contributions while you're still walking the earth?

Retirement is a tricky thing.

After decades of putting in a lot of hard work, I have one parent who retired at sixty-five and spends a ton of time helping friends and traveling as much as possible, and another who decided to keep working into his late seventies.

I have a husband who is eighteen years older than me and says he will never retire, no matter how many times people ask him if he's still working. "Yes, of course!" he says. His father retired at sixty-two, and Peter is convinced that he'd have lived longer had he kept working. It kept his mind sharp and gave him a real sense of purpose every day.

Then I have friends who are very entrepreneurial and share a goal of retiring at fifty-five (they're going to meet this objective). And I have a colleague who retired from law enforcement and finds himself busier than ever with multiple projects that draw on all his experience and wisdom. He's having a blast.

I also have friends who must keep working to make ends meet, regardless of being over sixty-five. "Pensions aren't what they used to be," and recent years of inflation have eaten into a fixed income household. Many Americans are going to work for a long time because of necessity or desire, so we have to find a way to make the most of it.

Another person I know made a significant amount of money from selling one company, planned to hang up his spurs and ski the world, but got so bored he started yet another company. Still other friends of mine are working into their eighties. And the chairman emeritus of Fox Corporation, Rupert Murdoch, shows up for work every day in his midnineties.

I have no idea what the right answer is on whether or when people should retire. Whereas mandatory retirements used to be the norm (and still are for some professions, like airline pilots), I think that retiring is a very personal decision. I find it a delicate subject.

So, let me share my thoughts for my own retirement plans: I have none! I just don't think about it. I love what I do, and I have bills to pay, and trips to take, and parties to throw. That all takes money. And I never think I'll have enough money to retire (though I recommend the book *Die with Zero* by Bill Perkins, to help deal with *that* natural anxiety).

Though one of my goals is to be healthy enough to do a long mission trip in Africa when I am ready to no longer do the work I'm doing now, I also have thought about teaching or mentoring in a more organized way. Part of me wants to be the ambassador to Tanzania (great country, lots of potential!). I want to travel and scour every inch of Spain, a country I love dearly. I want to take a big RV trip around America with

Peter and our dogs. (Yes, I said "dogs," plural, because when and if I retire, I absolutely want to have at least two dogs at once. One is amazing, but two would be ideal!) And I want to read novels. All the novels.

So, as you can see, I'm all over the map when it comes to retirement.

The best way to sort out questions about it was for me to ask others their thoughts.

Meantime, I'm going to start planning my retirement party. There will be chips and salsa! (And maybe even queso. But that's a long story.)

DAN BARR

Now that you've gotten over the hump and can look back and appreciate the many chapters of your life, what stands out to you?

It all goes very fast. I've heard older people say some version of this my whole life and I now know it is true. Careers are very important, and people should be thoughtful and purposeful in this regard, but it shouldn't be *the* most important thing.

I once read about a football coach in Maryland who would ask his senior players to write their own obituary. He asked them to really think about what they wanted their time on earth to have meant, what they wanted to be remembered for. I think there is a lot of wisdom in that. If you identify early on what your vision of a great, even heroic life is, you can and should set your sites on achieving that. Know who you are and let people feel the full weight of what you are bringing.

DAVID BAHNSEN

How do you define success and has that evolved throughout your life?

It definitely has evolved. I turn fifty next month, and I'm thinking about it even more these days.

Aristotle talked about the good life. There's the biblical idea of *shalom*. I use the term to connote peace and human flourishing and I believe it is both a material and spiritual, a physical and immaterial component where we have joy, prosperity, and harmony.

Success for me was never merely professional, but professional goals were (and are) a vital part of it.

Yet in the totality of my life, I care deeply that I am the best I am capable of being—that I produce all I can produce to the glory of my God—and that when I die He will say to me, "Well done, good and faithful servant." I am here to fight the good fight. I put that in my high school yearbook, and it is still true today even as a middle-aged man.

MARTHA MACCALLUM

How do you define success and has this evolved over time?

I was never driven by "success" in terms of money or recognition. But I always had and have a quiet driving inner force. To me to be successful is to be engaged, to be striving always, to be meeting new people and asking them questions, drawing them out about this life and history we are all part of.

For me the greatest success professionally has been

achieving a level where I have history and context to draw on from lived experiences and to share that with our audiences. I am covering my sixth presidential election, I've witnessed and covered the funerals and installations of popes, and the jubilees and funeral of a queen, the coronation of a king. I've walked in the footsteps of my eighteen-year-old uncle who died on the beaches of Iwo Jima. Those are the things that feel good to me.

DAVID BAHNSEN

How do you approach or advise people? Because I think you've already done this very well. But the balance of investing and saving for the future versus, say, not just paying your bills but enjoying the present.

Financially, you have to save off the top. The only way the government gets paid is they tax you off the top. The only way you get paid is if you save off the top (of your income).

So it's funny how these 401(k) things caused retirement balances to skyrocket higher. Live off percentages and put the mechanisms in place to make yourself do it. Some people live paycheck to paycheck—but where there is excess, get debt-free, and then be able to save 10 percent or 20 percent.

JACKIE DEANGELIS

What advice would you give someone who is new to investing and wants to start building wealth? When is it too early to start learning about financial responsibility?

Save, save, save! If you don't have money, you can't invest. The more money you have, the more you can try to grow it strategically. People think, "I don't make a lot, what's the point?" That's not true!

Financial responsibility starts from day one. I teach my clients everything from the value of a dollar to how to work to make a buck, then how to save it. I believe our financial future is actually determined in many cases by the example our parents set at home for us.

BRIAN BRENBERG

What advice would you give someone who is new to investing and wants to start building wealth? When is it too early to start learning about financial responsibility?

When to start teaching your kids about financial responsibility? Easy: the first time you stop for McDonald's and they complain that their friends' parents buy them sushi. Finance is the road from McDonald's to sushi.

When new to investing, one must learn how to budget so you can plan to save. You can't invest what you haven't set aside.

Get in the habit of putting money in the bank. Then take some of that and put it in a CD. Then take some of that and put it into a retirement savings vehicle. If you can accomplish all of that, you won't need my advice anymore.

TAYLOR RIGGS

What advice would you give someone who is new to investing and wants to start building wealth?

Start young and stay invested. Most people start too late because they are afraid they don't know what they are doing.

And when the market has a big correction, they get nervous and sell instead of staying invested.

My biggest piece of advice is "time in the market, not timing the market."

So invest in the market as young as you can—and hold on to your position for a very long time. I just bought an ETF that tracks the S&P 500 and dollar-cost average. I will try not to sell even when I'm nervous. And then I just hope that I build wealth by knowing the S&P 500 will be higher in twenty years than it is today.

TAYLOR RIGGS

When should you start teaching your kids about financial responsibility?

Yesterday! I believe it's never too early. I have a six-month-old daughter and I already talk to her out loud about budgeting when we are at the grocery store or what the markets did today or what earnings announcements are coming out next week. I tell her each paycheck how much I contributed to her 529 savings plan and I even opened up an investment account for her that includes money she got from family when she was born. I believe financial freedom is so important to teach her and help her feel comfortable in making smart financial choices.

JACKIE DEANGELIS

How do you approach the balance between investing and saving for the future versus enjoying the present?

First off, I take advantage of my 401(k) and the match, so

that comes off the top of my paycheck and I don't even think about it. Then I set a budget. I know exactly what comes in every month and what expenses are fixed. With the rest, I try to save half, if not more. And I always did this no matter how small my income was. Sometimes that means making hard choices and not doing something. But generally I feel I can do the things I want to do and still save.

TAYLOR RIGGS

How do you approach the balance between investing and saving for the future versus enjoying the present?

This is a tricky one. I truly believe in holding off on present purchases to invest in yourself and your family for the long term. But we have to feel happiness today. So I take a portion of my paycheck and put it in my 401(k) that I won't touch for thirty more years. Then I take another portion of my paycheck and use it to invest in stocks that I am interested in now. And then finally I take a small portion of my paycheck and save for a vacation or a dinner night out that my husband and I want to take together. But we can't eat out or go on a vacation if we also aren't saving for the future. That's our rule!

LAUREN FRITTS

When you look way ahead, what do you think of retirement? What would you want your colleagues and staff to feel about you at your retirement party?

Someone once shared with me the timeless adage, "It's never too late to be what you might have been." Instead of seeing retirement as a final chapter, I view it as an opportunity to explore new passions and ventures in my third and fourth acts of life. When that time comes, I'll be thinking, "What's next?"

I don't want to wait until my retirement party to gauge my team's feelings about me. We spend a lot of time on feedback. Feedback on projects and regular one-to-one. While we should balance negative with positive, we often wait for significant moments like retirement or leaving a company to exchange the real compliments. I think it's important to express appreciation more frequently than just at these milestones. Sometimes you don't realize the impact you've made until you hear it from others. When I left WeWork, the heartfelt notes I received were humbling, and it prompted me to reflect on what I want to bring to my next job.

So no matter where I go next or where I end up, I hope my colleagues saw my commitment to uplifting my team—bringing them to important meetings, seeking their input, and motivating them to realize their potential impact. I hope they can understand my passion extends beyond the task at hand or the company; it's about their success. Witnessing their growth and achievements brings me immense joy. I hope they feel this, and I encourage us all to seize moments and cherish feedback whenever it's shared—now and in the future.

PHIL LAGO

Retirement and beyond . . . What do you think is the key to a productive and meaningful retirement, and how do you plan to achieve it? How do you know when you're ready to retire, and what factors should people consider when making this decision?

Balance is crucial for both your life and business. Without it, one or both will suffer. If your business cannot function without you being there all the time, you need to reassess your team, perhaps hiring a COO with strengths to offset your weaknesses.

Prioritize personal wellness. Juggling work and social responsibilities can be stressful. Engage in hobbies, exercise, and healthy habits to refresh and reload mentally and physically. Encourage employee participation in a wellness program and lead by example. It may be a red flag if your career is the only passion in your life.

Get ready for retirement by planning emotionally, physically, and financially. Determine the top essential conditions for your ideal retirement, including location, access to excellent health care, and airport. Reassess and make data-rich, thoughtful decisions.

JESSE WATTERS

When you think ahead, what do you want Jesse Watters's legacy to be?

I'd like to be remembered as a man of strong character who is kind and did good things for his family, friends, and country.

FRANK SILLER

Do you think about retiring? And what do you think about next chapters for people who might want to move on from their first or second career and into their later years in order to keep active and productive?

Retirement isn't a concept I entertain often; there's so much more to achieve through the foundation. For others contemplating their next chapters, I see it as an opportunity to redefine their lives. Engaging in activities that fulfill not just personal ambitions but also contribute to the welfare of others can provide a deeply satisfying and vibrant later life.

JOHN ROBERTS

How do you think about next chapters in your career? Do you think about what's next or have you learned to just take the days and years as they come?

At this point, I am so happy with what I'm doing that I haven't thought of what comes next. I suppose at some point, I could hang it up and hit the golf course, but I am many years away from making that decision. One thing I do notice, though: the years are going by more quickly than I could have ever imagined.

PETER MCMAHON

Retirement. It's long been a strong no for you. Why is that? How do you think about winding down huge workloads to be able to enjoy more of the other things you do in life?

When I was in my early forties I had a plan to semiretire at fifty-five, get a part-time gig doing consulting or something similar. Then by the time I was in my sixties it had lost its appeal. And now at seventy I don't relish the thought at all. Okay, I do have a startup business with a great partner and friend, so my job is not just work. In many ways it's like a hobby. I interact with (mostly) people I like and enjoy the process. I will confess the regulatory aspects of surgical devices don't excite me, but I do wake up every morning ready to go.

When I was about forty-five, I recall being in Dubai and a gentleman there I met was seventy and attending the trade show. I recall thinking, "I don't want to be trailing round the world on business when I'm seventy." Well, now I'm seventy and frankly I still enjoy traveling round the world and doing business with people I mostly like, many of whom have been friends for several years or even decades. I find it to be mentally very stimulating.

I know a number of people who have retied early and, whether they admit it or not, are clearly rather bored, finding things to do to pass the time rather than finding the time to do things you want to get done. Now, this is certainly not the case for everyone, which is fine, but I like to have a distinct purpose in my day. And I have it balanced where I have a long walk with the dog in the morning, have time to play tennis a few times a week in the summer, and spend a good deal of time with Dana at our home on the beach—and still enjoying all the other things I do in life.

STUART VARNEY

We have talked about the R-word. Retirement. You're crushing it now just as you have for years. How do you think about retirement now? Any advice for others who are thinking about their next steps?

Funny you should ask! I will be seventy-six in a few weeks and of course, the question of retirement comes up constantly. I have to consider three things: First, what would

I do if I were no longer working? Second, would I miss doing my show? Third, how would my family react to having me "underfoot" 24/7?

If you read between the lines, you can probably understand that I am highly conflicted, but I think I'm leaning toward continuing to work.

Of course, lurking in the background are the questions of health and attitude. If your health doesn't stand up, the decision has been made for you. As for attitude, I'm trying to work out if I really want to keep on pushing myself to get up every morning at 2:45 a.m. and go to bed at night at 7:30 and walk away from any kind of social life. Stay tuned. This debate inside my head will go on for a long time!

PAUL MAURO

Could you describe your experience in deciding to retire from the NYPD and then finding that you have so many transferable skills and could go in many different directions? And how did you find that experience? Do you have any advice for others considering going through the same thing?

Police work and intelligence work, the two things I would consider my main professional capabilities, don't necessarily transfer well to the private sector. The world is filled with ex-cops doing security work that may pay, but which the retirees rarely find as fulfilling as their years "on the job." And that job sector is flooded.

I had the benefit of a number of family members who had done various forms of government security work, so I knew the paradigm. How, then, to get out ahead of it?

My own tack was to "add a hat." What I mean is, I wanted

to add some sort of an overlay to my police experience that would make me something more than another "ex-cop." In my case, I chose law school, which I attended at night.

Was it hard? An anecdote:

It was my job to deliver a daily brief to several NYPD commissioners of intelligence for many years, and sometimes to the police commissioner. These were all extremely smart, accomplished men. Facing tough questions from them, a soft shoe wouldn't cut it.

So I had to stay single-minded. I read all the time (I eventually ended up needing reading glasses). I read investigative summaries on my BlackBerry on the subway, I read law school briefs before going to sleep and on meals, I listened to legal outlines on compact disks in my car (I'm aware I'm dating myself here).

Now, no one knew any of this. I kept it to myself, so it wouldn't look like I was distracted (and truthfully, I was not). But to be honest, I also kept it quiet in case I had to drop out.

Entering my final school year, when I eventually had to reveal it—I'd been chosen for an internship in a federal prosecutor's office, and word of that would undoubtedly get around—many people asked me, "How have you been managing all this?"

My answer: "The commissioner knows about 50 percent of what goes on in my shop. If I know 51 percent, I look like a genius."

Now, I knew a hell of a lot more than 51 percent. But the point: Add a hat, sure. Plan for your next move. But make sure to feed the beast. Never neglect your current job while enhancing your future prospects.

Which also means, if at all possible, pick something that enhances your value to your *current* job. That's why I chose law school. It made me more valuable in the future, sure. But it also helped me punch at a much higher weight in my current job.

It broadened me, I believe. To others and in truth, to myself.

Chapter 7: Dana's Takeaways

- Start young and stay invested so that you have the ability to make decisions about retirement with freedom.

- Think of next chapters after your career. What else would you love to accomplish or see? What sport of skill have you always wanted to try?

- There is so much talent, experience, and wisdom in an older worker. Harness that to keep organizations successful.

- Work to take care of your health. It is not something you can delegate!

CHAPTER 8

What Is the Best Advice You've Ever Gotten?

When I started Minute Mentoring, I knew I didn't have all the answers. But the one thing I definitely know how to do is find the right people to ask. One of my favorite questions for mentors is, "What is the best advice you've ever received?"

Below are some of the greatest responses I've gotten:

What is the best advice you've been given, and what is your favorite piece of advice to give?

DIERKS BENTLEY

"Keep flowin', keep creatin', don't think too much, let's go, baby!"

Coach Chippy, an avid hockey fan and Instagram guy, left me that message in a funny Canadian hockey coach voice.

But I think it applies really well to life in general. You have to keep flowing with life, regardless of what it throws at you, and you need to keep creating and following your bliss. When possible, don't overthink things, put the work in, trust the process, be present in the moment.

And lastly, have fun!

MICHELE CHASE

Don't talk just for the sake of talking.

I was at a pivotal time in my career and a former CFO of mine said this to me. I tended to think out loud when I was younger and thought I should always have an answer. It's okay to be thoughtful and come back with an answer or to seek counsel from a trusted colleague or mentor to make sure you're not missing anything.

Sometimes it's okay to say you need to sleep on it and come back to them. Just always make sure you circle back to close the loop. People come to me with complicated things, which is why they are asking in the first place!

My other favorite piece of advice to give is *that people don't care how much you know; they want to know how much you care.*

TOM SHILLUE

Keep a diary.

I don't even remember who told me this—it was an athlete who came to speak at an event at my high school. A former New England Patriot, or someone from the Red Sox or the Celtics maybe regretted not keeping a diary when he was in high school, and there were so many things he'd forgotten.

And I remember he said, "Write something every day, and don't worry about what you're writing—you can just write what you had for breakfast."

If a teacher or principal had said it I might have ignored it, but this guy was a pro athlete, so the next day I started a diary. I still have it, and it's a treasure trove of memories that I surely would have forgotten otherwise.

MORA NEILSON

Today is the tomorrow you worried about yesterday. (I saw it hanging over a bar in Newport, Rhode Island, and will never forget it.)

Also: Take the job. You're better than you think you are.

MARTHA MACCALLUM

Read and learn.

My mom was a teacher, and she loved learning. She never stopped reading, and every time we were together or even apart, she would share with me an article, her thoughts on a book she just read. If I asked her about something she didn't know, she'd often look it up and send me what she found, copied and printed in the mail, with a note. She loved to talk with people and she gave them her attention. She was there when someone needed her, family or friend.

So her life was the best advice. I encourage people to never stop growing. Life is too short. Always "want to know."

Also: get outside a lot. When you're in trouble, go for a long walk and think it through. Ask God to show you the way. Seek knowledge. Embrace joy.

BILL HEMMER

Be humble. My mom always said it.

GREG GUTFELD

Wow, that's a hard one. I guess the best advice is to know when someone just gave you great advice.

Which means making yourself available to hear it. There are those who won't hear advice. Those are the people who think they're always right, and everything done could always have been better if we only listened to him! So let me think and rattle off some . . .

- **Write for the reader, not for you.** Over time both goals will coalesce. But write as though you're writing an instruction manual. Basic English, direct, simple. Everyone wants to be better, and if you deliver concise instructions, they value that most. Channel your personal desires for accolades elsewhere.

- **Create a system, not a goal.** This is a Scott Adams invention. If you have a goal without a system, the goal will not be met. But if you have a system—a regular pattern of doing things every day—even if you don't reach the magical goal, you will achieve many things along the way. And sooner or later, a new better goal appears, or the old one is forgotten. But the system is there always. So, a good example of system versus goals:

o **Writing every day versus writing the great American novel.** I would love to achieve that goal, but instead I took a job early on, writing every day for a mass-market health magazine. And I kept writing and writing. I've written ten books, and thousands upon thousands of TV scripted segments. I will write that novel when I'm good and ready, but what an amazing body of work that system created. The goal didn't do that.

o **Exercising and eating wisely versus wanting to lose fifty pounds.** When people set a massive goal, it's so overwhelming they just figure "what's the use" and keep eating until they hate themselves more. But just a system of regular exercise (starting slow) and diet (eliminating one thing at a time) and slowly you find it happening, and the incremental results actually give you a better sense of satisfaction than if suddenly that fifty pounds were to disappear. The weird thing about sudden success (liposuction or Ozempic) is that it always leads to a return of what you vanquished. But if you put the effort into it—the pain—then you're less likely to betray all that work. You won't gain the weight back because you're betraying the "you" from yesterday while punishing the "you" of tomorrow.

PATTI CALLAHAN HENRY

"Grant me the serenity to accept the things I cannot change. The courage to change the things I can. And the wisdom to know the difference."

Ask the beautiful questions about these things from the Serenity Prayer. What can we change? What is not ours to change and control? Do I have the courage and wisdom to know the difference?

The lifelong quest for the answers is paramount for me to live well with uncertainty, contradictions, and the paradox of mystery.

MIKE ROWE

"Get yourself a different toolbox."

This came from Grandfather, when I realized at sixteen years of age that the "handy gene" was recessive, and that I had not inherited his natural ability to build, repair, or fabricate anything with my own two hands.

I was devastated, but he knew exactly what I needed to hear. "You can be a tradesman," he said, "if that's really what you want to be. Just get yourself a different toolbox."

I was determined to follow in my grandfather's footsteps. But of course, just because you love something, doesn't mean you can't suck at it.

And that's why, in spite of my thoughts on risk and curiosity, which I think apply to everyone, I'm pretty stingy with offering advice to the masses. I think a lot of people have been adversely impacted by the preponderance of one-size-fits-all, cookie-cutter conventional wisdom that seems to permeate every topic today.

We're told, for instance, by lots of well-intended people, to pursue our goals with "persistence and determination," and to "always stay the course."

But that only makes sense if you're headed in the right direction, and I have no idea if you are. Hopefully you have a grandfather or a parent or a trusted friend to help you figure that out.

SALENA ZITO

Stop trying to run with a crowd you don't belong in—this came from an editor when I initially thought that I should be on the campaign bus with all the other "big-time" journalists.

I had called him from a phone booth in Scranton, Pennsylvania, in tears, frustrated because the campaign bus was an awful experience, we hadn't been allowed to talk to voters, we were essentially cut off from the experience, and everyone seemed to be writing the same story.

I thought that if this is what I was supposed to do to be successful and if this is what success is, I don't want to do it. Nothing felt real.

That was when he told me to stop trying to run with a crowd I didn't belong in and asked me what I thought I should be doing. I told him I thought it would be better to break free from the bus and cover it from a voter's perspective. I've been doing it that way ever since.

JACKIE DEANGELIS

Stop caring what people think about you!

Easier said than done. But this is freeing.

The minute I realized the people that are judging me aren't paying my bills or walking in my shoes, I became very empowered to make the right choices for myself on a daily basis.

BRIAN BRENBERG

The more you trust in the grace of God and not your own striving, the freer you will be to pursue much more than you ever imagined.

TAYLOR RIGGS

Be kind to yourself (we are our own worst critics) and give yourself a lot of grace during your growing pains. Have faith that life will all work out how it is meant to be.

TREY GOWDY

Never assume everyone wants to see you do well.

That is a hard lesson to learn. Humans are capable of great jealousy.

Related: Be humble, because sometimes even your friends do not want to see you succeed "too much."

Then let's move to what two Speakers of the House told me about politics, which is "It's better to be a good person with a bad idea, than a bad person with a good idea."

Now we can move to what yet another Speaker of the

House told me, which is "Find what you are good at, do that. Don't do the rest."

What he meant was find where you can help the team, master that. Do not try to commandeer where others are or usurp their opportunities.

SANDRA SMITH

I run a lot with my son now and the best advice I have ever gotten now comes from him: "You got this, Mom."

LAWRENCE JONES

1. "Remember, this is show business, not show friends."

2. "Enjoy the journey."

JIMMY FAILLA

Make excellence your goal in everything you do.

If you strive to attain it every day, you will become undeniable in your field, at which point time will become the great equalizer between where you are and where you want to be.

It took me twenty years to get where I am but I wouldn't trade any of it for anything in the world. (Okay, I'd probably be willing to part with the smell of my taxi, but you get the point.)

ANDREA ARAGON

1. "Just be you."
   This simple bit of advice hit me like a ton of bricks.

Why? Perhaps, in this crazy world, we have forgotten how to be our authentic selves. Like most, I was always comparing myself to others, absorbed in my short-comings rather than my strengths. It never occurred to me that my perspective could be exactly what was needed. Once I learned to accept that just being "me" was actually a good thing, it had a profound impact on me. I was only able to grow more as an individual and person of value from there. When I think I am not enough, I hear these words in my head, and I feel free.

2. Do what you say you are going to do.

That is it! Simply follow through on your words and commitments through your actions and you will miraculously find yourself ahead of the rest. You might be surprised to find this is a rare skill, but believe me, it is.

BRIAN KILMEADE

Networking is key. The people you meet who can impact your career should be cherished. It's always best to get advice or meet people without asking them for a job or a favor. Successful people get that all day. Always send handwritten thank-you notes for the time and advice. Make them short and legible, always including a card or number for someone to reach you.

The best axiom that's held up since the day I heard it: you can judge a person's character by how they treat people they need nothing from.

Also, if you know of good people going through a rough

time, reaching out to support them is always so appreciated. That's when real people of integrity show themselves.

JESSICA TARLOV

"If it won't matter five years from now, don't worry about it today."

Life changes so quickly and planning too much for an uncertain future holds so many people back. The small stuff is actually small and not worth the anxiety.

LAUREN FRITTS

1. **"Give yourself grace."** It's a reminder that we're all human and bound to make mistakes. We are often told to be empathetic to others but never toward ourselves. In the field of communications, where control is often emphasized, accepting that not everything is within our power can be liberating. We strive for perfection, but it's essential to recognize that sometimes outcomes are beyond our control. Giving ourselves grace allows us to navigate uncertainties with resilience and compassion.

2. **"It's okay to care."** It's easy to get caught up in a mission, but I believe it's more important to genuinely care—about the work you do and the people you work with. Whether in national TV shows, politics, or office spaces, I've always found a reason to care in every place I've worked. Often, it's because of our team

and the remarkable people I've had the privilege to work alongside, which fueled my determination to keep pushing forward. Everyone can and should find a reason to care; it makes work much more fulfilling.

3. **"You'll never know if you don't ask."** Just ask. Want to know why someone made that call? Want to go on that TV shoot? Want to be a part of an important meeting? Don't wait to be invited or told "why." You'll learn more and achieve more by seeking answers and opportunities. If it's not appropriate to ask, you'll learn from the experience and grow from it.

   The best opportunities in my life have arisen because I dared to ask to get involved in projects or sit at the table. Ambition is often perceived as overly ambitious, but in reality, most people's ambition is simply expressed through asking questions in an effort to learn and grow.

DR. MARK SHRIME

1. Wear out, don't rust out.

2. Work at being the best at where you are *right now*. If you're always looking to what comes next, you'll miss a lot of what's happening. Be present.

PHIL LAGO

Most important piece of advice: make the organization better, not just yourself.

Be yourself, but be open to growth, learning, and teaching. Mistakes are opportunities for improvement, not lifelong sentences. Focus on being hardworking, reliable, adaptable, and goal-oriented. The rest will fall into place. Learn a skill-set which is valuable to the organization and become the expert. Work hard to understand organizational dynamics. Also, understand that your "job" is to make those around you better. Pease don't let fear hold you back; relax and enjoy the journey. It won't be a straight line and that is okay.

JESSE WATTERS

1. The Stoics talk about using your natural gift of reason to master your emotions. Being dominated and driven by your emotions, your anger, your fear, your base desires, and your passions is not the way to live a virtuous life. Look around at the people who overindulge, submit to addictions, seek pleasure every moment, or waste their lives and comfort. These are unhappy, anxious, volatile people. A life of self-discipline, moderation, reflection, industriousness, and proper planning will bring happiness, joy, and success.

2. Life is about good decisions. Everyone's life is the result of every single decision they've ever made. Each moment is an opportunity for you to make a decision. Are you going to read or watch TV? Are you going to eat junk or eat healthy? Are you going to exercise or lie around? Are you going to work or procrastinate? Are you going to listen or talk over

someone? If you can create a life for yourself of good habits, you will live a virtuous life. Commit to these habits daily and don't break them until they become second nature. Wake up early, get outside. Drink water. Exercise. Read, write, reflect, breathe, work. Eat eggs, fish, salad, and meat. Do cold plunge and sauna. Stay in the moment and don't let negative thoughts enter your mind.

FRANK SILLER

1. "While we have time, let us do good." This advice from my father has shaped my life's mission and the core philosophy of the Tunnel to Towers Foundation.

2. Live a life of service. The fulfillment you gain from serving others enriches your life far more than any material success ever could. It creates legacies of love and resilience that outlast your time on earth.

PETER MCMAHON

"Keep your eye on the ball."

Certainly for hand-eye sports, especially tennis, but metaphorically throughout life. Try and determine where that ball of fate is headed, how fast, if it's spinning or curving, and just how high it will bounce—if it does.

STUART VARNEY

You won't be happy unless your spouse is happy.

BENJAMIN HALL

It's never too late. It's never too late to start something, it's never too late to repair something, it's never too late to improve something, it's never too late to change something. You can do anything you want and you can start it right now. Don't let the end goal become your only focus—enjoy the journey itself, both the ups and the downs. Mistakes are fine too.

JEANINE PIRRO

The best advice I've ever received is to never put a piece of paper down once you have read it. Either make a decision, do research, seek advice, or do whatever you have to. Resolve the issue, never put it away for another time, or it will only add stress to your already burdened schedules.

The advice I would pass on is to remember not only to do a great job, but to conduct yourself in a way that complements that job. Your reputation is everything; respect it, preserve it, and fight for it.

PAUL MAURO

Head down, mouth shut, eyes open.

AINSLEY EARHARDT

1. "Trust in the Lord with all your heart and lean not on your own understanding; in all your ways submit to him, and he will make your paths straight"

(Proverbs 3:5–6). Put your faith first and God will determine your steps.

2. Most people ask me how I reached success because they want to do the same. And I always tell them the same advice. Work harder than everyone else, put in the effort, and enjoy your journey. Even if you are broke or in a position you don't necessarily want, keep fighting for the job you do want. Treat the job you have as if it's the best job and say yes to every opportunity your boss provides. Have a good attitude and be thankful.

BRET BAIER

Best advice I was given: don't let anyone tell you what you can or can't do. If you believe you can do something, trust yourself over anyone else. I change that to say, "Keep driving no matter if you don't know how you're going to get to your destination. Sometimes you can't see the whole road ahead, but if you keep driving, eventually you will get there."

STEVE DOOCY

After I graduated from college and was working as a TV reporter in Topeka making four dollars an hour, I was struggling financially. My parents struggled when I was growing up, but they had each other and kids to struggle with them. I was struggling all by myself, in Topeka. I didn't want to tell them how bad it was; besides, they didn't have an extra nickel to send my way, although they'd find one if I asked.

A work friend suggested I read the book *The Road Less Traveled*. The first line of the book grabbed me in its simplicity and clarity: "Life is difficult." No kidding.

The author, M. Scott Peck, then explained what I was precisely feeling, but then gave me the key to a different outlook. He wrote, "Once we truly know that life is difficult—once we truly understand and accept it, then life is no longer difficult. Because once it is accepted, the fact that life is difficult no longer matters."

Suddenly I realized I was not the only one who had those feelings, and it was liberating. I was still living on Morton pot pies that were sale priced ten for one dollar, but at least I knew I had plenty of company.

So my advice to young people is just know that life takes effort. Nobody tells you that when you're a kid; otherwise nobody would ever leave home. Just know if you only want to do what's easy, life will probably be tough. If you want to be successful in a job, just know nobody is going to give you anything, unless you are going into the family business, but even there a blood relative might snap at you during inventory to stop watching cat videos on your work computer.

Good luck!

CHAPTER 9

Dana's Dos and Don'ts

(What I Learned Along the Way . . .)

By now you've realized how much there is to learn from others' experiences—and how you can always be learning (ABL) from them. I know I learned a lot from listening to their examples and stories. Writing this book was a reminder to me that it's good to be curious, as Mike Rowe told us in Chapter 1. We should always ask people about how they got where they are, what their journey was like, and what they learned over the years that can help inspire, reassure, or encourage us to make decisions or changes. It's also a smart way to realize that hey, you're actually on the right track and that everything will actually be okay.

In this chapter, our education continues with a few bits of advice, some stories, and many things I wish someone had told me along the way. It's a superefficient chapter where you can get a lot of information. Read it in full or in bits and pieces. And be sure to take notes—there might be a quiz. (You know I love a quiz.)

BETTER SAY GREAT

In 2020, Fox broadcast the Super Bowl. It was also the beginning of the election year. Busy was an understatement. Many of us at Fox News had to travel from Miami to Iowa to Washington, D.C., to New Hampshire, all in one week. This was the most difficult trip to pack for in my lifetime—sun, snow and ice, high heels and boots, several outfits for TV, and don't forget the pajamas!

Our morning call time for leaving Miami was 4 a.m. That meant everyone needed to be up, packed, and ready to depart for the airport for the flight to Iowa.

The night before, I'd been a real party pooper and gone to bed at 9 p.m. I didn't even stay up to watch the game. I still don't know who won. What's a football look like, anyway?

I stayed in because I knew that I needed to pace myself to make it through the ten days of coverage. Others stayed out late and had a big night. My assistant was one of them.

I was in the lobby early. (Of course I was. I run early to everything, which really helped when I worked for President Bush, who often liked to start meetings well before the appointed time.)

Brian Kilmeade knew my assistant had been out on the town. As she walked up to join the group, he asked her, "How are you doing?"

I jumped in and said, "Better say great!"

And she said, "Great!"

Even if she didn't mean it, I appreciated that attitude so much. She powered through that day on the little sleep she had, and I was so proud of her. That's my girl!

Each morning on *America's Newsroom*, my co-anchor, Bill

Hemmer, and I are constantly asking how the other is doing. We laugh as we say in unison, "Better say great!"

Your attitude about how you're doing matters. You get to choose how you answer, and while no one should shy away from their true feelings, faking it until you're making it can go a long way with the boss.

YOU NEVER GET IN TROUBLE FOR SOMETHING YOU DIDN'T SAY

During White House press briefings, there were so many times I thought of a sarcastic quip that would have made a reporter look foolish or at least have provided my team with a good laugh.

I almost always suppressed it. I would imagine President Bush watching the briefing and wondering if he would be proud of me at that moment. And if the answer was no, then I didn't say it. Sometimes I'd take it back with me for the post briefing venting session and we'd chuckle about it there. (Safely, where no one else would hear us.)

This reminds me of one of the best pieces of advice I've ever heard. It came from Vice President Dick Cheney.

Once I read an interview with him about how the vice president let everyone in the room express themselves before he did, so that each person would feel comfortable offering their opinion instead of hiding it thinking that he wouldn't approve. He wanted all the ideas and opinions expressed so that he could digest them before weighing in. This is a smart approach for any leader.

I asked him about that one time and said I admired his ability to listen.

He said, "There's another good reason not to talk all the time: You never get in trouble for something you didn't say."

This is such good advice. Whether swallowing a joke at someone else's expense, a comment that would stifle debate, or spreading gossip that may not be true, resisting the urge to say it out loud can make a huge, discerning difference.

This goes for emails and text messages too.

If a comment is really burning a hole in your draft folder, don't send it, but save it for a trusted colleague or friend.

Have the laugh.

But keep it to yourselves.

CAN YOU TAKE A PUNCH?

"They want to see if you can take a punch and get up off the mat and punch back," President Bush said once when the 2008 primary was underway. He was talking about the other candidates, the media, and the voters.

Everyone expects a fight and respects someone who can fight back with finesse, humor, and charm.

You may never run for office, but over the years you'll take a punch. Maybe you'll lose a client pitch to a competitor, get dropped by a boyfriend, or miss out on a big promotion. Perhaps you'll deal with all of those in one short week.

You could be laid out flat. So, now what?

The worst thing you can do is wallow in your mistakes or disappointments. You'll waste time and energy replaying it over and over: "I should have said this or that. I will never get that promotion now, and I am going to be alone for the rest of my life." That's the kind of negativity that holds you back until you let it go.

I heard a story once about a little boy who was a very good piano player at his first recital. He had one easy piece that he could play in his sleep, no problem. Then he had a harder piece that was a showcase and would hopefully help him win the competition.

He took his seat on the piano bench and started to play the easy song. And he messed up. He froze for a second and the audience cringed for him. He tried to power through, but instead of losing his cool, getting mad, or crying, he did something I think was very brave. He stopped. Took a deep breath, gathered himself, and then started over from the beginning. He found a way to work out his nerves and salvage his performance.

We're all going to find times when we need to muster our resilience. And if you're not the one needing to get up off the mat, can you help someone who does? Reach down and lift them up. They'll never forget it, and you'll build up some down-on-your-luck capital in your good-friend account.

ALWAYS PASS ON A COMPLIMENT

I try to live by a motto of always passing on a compliment. It's an enjoyable habit.

As humans, we tend only to remember the negative things that are said about us—a bad outfit, a crack in our voice, a lapse in judgment. We almost never remember the compliments or the positive events. The negatives take up way too much space in our brains.

Knowing this, I started a new note in the app on my phone on New Year's Day. It was titled "Nice Things Said About Me This Year."

I wanted to hold on to a kind word or two that would help

me when I was feeling down. A list I could look back on at the end of the year to make me happy.

As I was writing this book, I remembered that note. I pulled out my phone to look it up. Guess what?

It was blank.

I mean, surely someone had to have said something nice about me, right?

Well, even if they had, it didn't matter one bit—I was too busy focusing on the negatives, the things I could do better, the items on my to-do list, etc.

This is why it's important to keep up my habit of at least passing on compliments to other people. Even if they don't write it down, it will give them a little boost.

While we're on the subject, let me say one thing nice about you right now: you're so wise to be reading this book!

CLARITY, DIGNITY, GRACE

When I was a kid, *Dry Idea* deodorant had a tagline that said, "Never let them see you sweat."

One of the ways to do that is to live by a personal code of ethics. That way you can handle adversity without letting anyone see concerns or worries.

I observed this from my grandfather, Leo E. Perino. To me he was so gracious, kind, warm, tough, wise, and funny. A World War II Marine veteran, a rancher, and a devoted husband. His way of life—working the land, handing out advice to other ranchers, and modeling integrity and intelligence—was like a tale out of a western storybook. He was a great role model and taught me that preparedness, plus hard work and an open heart, combine to make for a happier life.

I also learned more about this from President Bush. He often talked about how living based on a set of principles made decision-making much easier.

For example, if you live by a moral code, then you won't find yourself in compromising situations. It simplifies your life. And I'm all for that! Less drama and more happiness are what I'm always going for.

Living by a code means you can hold your head high, even if the decision you make is unpopular. So, you have to sit alone at the lunch table for a while? That's okay. It's worth it.

Think about it. Would you rather be sitting alone or feel sick to your stomach that you violated your own personal code? That you couldn't look yourself in the mirror and be proud of what you see?

Your dignity is worth so much. And you must protect your integrity at all costs. This will be the most personal investment you make in your lifetime. And it's truly all up to you. No one else can do that for you.

So, chin up, shoulders back. When you lead with your principles, you will stand taller and more comfortable in your own skin.

SEE SOMETHING, SAY SOMETHING

I still get an upset stomach when I think about how I could have prevented a major problem for President Bush in 2006.

I was a junior deputy in the press office and had noticed an item in a small news outlet that would likely rile up the Congress. I mentioned it to the press secretary but was told it was fine and not going to come up at the briefing.

The next day, the issue was on the front page of that paper. I raised it a second time. Again I was told to let it go. My gut told me it was potentially a big deal, but I wasn't as experienced as others and sat back meekly but unsettled.

While I thought for a moment about quietly going above the press secretary's head to mention it to the chief of staff, I didn't. I was scared to do it—to be seen as a worrywart with bad judgment and overreacting.

Well, the next day the issue exploded all over the media, and it caused a firestorm that last three weeks and earned the president's first veto threat.

I could just crawl under my desk as I type this nearly twenty years later.

So take it from me: If you see something at the office that concerns you, raise it. And if your immediate supervisor isn't responsive and you still think there's a potential problem, find a way to appeal or to get the concern heard by someone higher up the food chain. Be smart about it. But do it.

This is especially important for public safety and can help prevent public relations nightmares as well.

YOU *ARE* THE NET

I've always had a bit of financial anxiety. Even after achieving a level of career success and decent investments, I worry that it could all disappear tomorrow morning when I wake up.

I think part of this has to do with feeling like I'm walking on a high wire without a net. That I have to get every step just right or I could fall.

When I get overwhelmed like that, I like to talk to my friend Ingrid Henrichsen. We met at a barre class on Fifty-Seventh Street and became sister-friends immediately. She's wise, thoughtful, beautiful, funny, and supportive.

I remember telling her how I felt about being up on that high wire and worrying that there was nothing below to break a fall.

She said, "Dana, you *are* the net. Don't you see? *You* are the net."

Wow! Bam! Pow!

She was right. I am the net.

I have proven that I can succeed, handle adversity, overcome obstacles. I can pick myself up if something goes wrong. I am an educated, American woman with a loving husband, terrific friends, and a job I love. All that combines to make a strong net.

I've never worried about that since.

I am the net.

Be your own net. Build that strength in yourself.

Thank you, Ingrid.

FINANCIAL WELLNESS

Financial literacy is critical to having a more comfortable and enjoyable life. In America we don't teach this enough and so people get into the workforce and try to figure it out on their own.

There are some good books, websites, and podcasts that can help you. I recommend the following:

- *Unbreakable Inventory*, by Charles Payne

- *The Money Book for the Young, Fabulous, and Broke*, by Suze Orman

- *The Little Book of Commonsense Investing*, by John C. Boyle

  There are also some great podcasts, including:

- *We Make Money Fun*

- *How to Money*

- *The Personal Finance Podcast*

- *Money Girl*

- *Wealthy After Forty*

- *The Dave Ramsey Show*

Because I am not an expert and have worked to overcome some money anxiety as an adult, I asked my trusted advisor from Morgan Stanley, Norbert Frassa, to give me his top advice for financial wellness. His answers are so good, I decided to provide them in full below. What follows are Norbert's top tips.

FINANCIAL CALORIES WITH NORBERT FRASSA

1. **Write down your financial goals.** Antoine de Saint-Exupéry said, "A goal without a plan is just a wish."

We all have great intentions when it comes to our money, but we are more likely to achieve our financial goals if we write them down. It does not stop at just writing down your goals. You also need to come up with specific accountable activities that move you toward your target.

Take some time to visualize the life you want. Now think of the money that you need to get you there. Finally, how much do you have to earn, save, or invest so you can get closer each month? There will be times when things go wrong, but having a solid plan in black and white is key to keeping you on track.

Bonus Tip—Keep your written goals in a place you will see them every day like your refrigerator door or dressing mirror. You can do it!

2. **Understand the power of compounding.** Would you rather get a million dollars today or would you rather get a penny today that doubles in value every day for thirty days? Well, if you chose the million dollars you made a good choice today, but in thirty days you would regret your decision. That penny that doubled each day would have grown to over $5 million. That is the power of compounding.

How many times have you heard, "Oh, I will start that tomorrow." With investing, the secret sauce is starting today. The longer you allow your investments to grow, the more time they will have to appreciate in value. Small steps are okay too. If you do not have enough to save $100 per month, then save $25 per month and build from there. Time is money.

3. **Early in your life, spending money should be painful.** What will you have to do if you want to be physically fit? You must reduce your number of net calories of course! That includes reducing the number of calories that come from your food each week. Keeping track of what you eat will definitely help, but it is not easy.

   The same is true with financial fitness. Reducing your expenses is like keeping track of those financial calories. Our world is set up to make things easy and that includes paying for things. If you tap your phone to buy something, it does not feel painful at all. But over time, how do you know where your money is going? How many financial calories are you eating?

   Keep track of your expenses. You can use a pencil and paper, a spreadsheet, or an online tool that you trust. Review everything critically, especially monthly subscriptions. Do you have a streaming subscription for that show that you do not watch anymore? Save that money.

   Bonus Tip—Do not automate your payments. This might seem counterintuitive, but manually paying your bills each month at this stage in your life lets you feel the pain of money going out.

4. **Set up savings to automatically go into an account before it hits your checking account.** You

say to yourself, "I am responsible and going to pay all my bills then I will save whatever is leftover." It will probably never happen. You need to learn to pay yourself first.

You *should not* automate your payments to others, but you *should* automate that payment to you and your savings or investment account. It should be the first place your money goes each pay period. The future you will thank you.

5. **If you get a promotion, increase your savings before the first paycheck hits.** Congratulations! You just got promoted and got a big raise. You might say to yourself, What should I buy first? A new purse? A new laptop?

   The best thing to do is bump up your monthly savings before you get used to extra money hitting your bank account. If we see money in our checking account, we tend to spend it. If you increased your savings first, your will be able to conquer those long-term targets quicker. You have those goals written down, right?

6. **Set up a Roth IRA as soon as you start working and making money.** One of the best ways to start investing is by using an account that is called a Roth IRA. When you get a job, you can fund this account each year up to an annual limit. A Roth IRA will allow your money to grow tax-free if you leave the money invested in the account until age fifty-nine and a half for your retirement. Plus, you could withdraw the

money that you put into the account for an emergency without a penalty.

Bonus Tip—If your employer offers you a match on your contributions to their retirement plan, take advantage of that too. It is free money that you can use for retirement.

7. **Get used to living on 90 percent of your income.** Typically a person's income grows as they get older with more work experience. As you start your career, it can be difficult to make ends meet and living paycheck to paycheck can be common.

   However, there is not much difference in your overall lifestyle if you learn to live with only 90 percent of your income. The first 10 percent of your paycheck should be going toward building a savings account and investing.

8. **Social media is not your friend.** Social media allows us to stay connected with our family and friends to see what is new in their lives. However, it also drives impulsive behavior. So sometimes we see the extravagant meal that our friends had last night. Or the expensive outfit that our coworker is wearing today. Not only that, but the social media companies are inserting ads every chance they can.

   This type of activity can not only easily spend your time, but it can easily spend your funds. It is important to use our hard-earned money because it brings us happiness and not just because we saw it online and want it too. In addition, the newest viral thing that everyone is buying right now might not be the best use of your money.

9. **Learn to use credit cards wisely.** Everyone gets lots of offers to apply for credit cards. These companies know that if you become their customer early in life, there is a good chance you will be their customer for the rest of it.

It is crucial that you know that credit card interest is one of the easiest ways to destroy wealth. If you cannot pay off the balance in full each month, then you should not be putting expenses on a credit card. The yearly interest rates on credit cards can go higher than 30 percent APR in some cases.

Bonus Tip—Making 100 percent on-time payments is the biggest factor in getting a good FICO score. Never miss a payment on any debts.

10. **Invest in yourself.** If you genuinely want to live your best life and do well financially, *you* are the best thing in which to invest your time and money! Continue learning, building solid networking and support groups, and stretching yourself to try new things. The easiest way to increase your net worth is to increase your income.

Remember that money is a tool and not a destination. Not everything will go in your favor and that's okay. However, if you remain determined and consistent, money can allow you to have the freedom and flexibility in life that you deserve. You've got what it takes!

SOCIAL MEDIA SMARTS

Here's a good rule: if you don't want your mom to see something you are about to post, then don't do it.

Have a private shared photo album for pictures and videos that are borderline? Why cross it and risk your boss or colleagues seeing something that could reflect poorly on you in the future?

Employers, colleagues, and networking contacts are going to look up the person they're about to meet or that they're about to interview. Fair or not, that's the way it is. Your visual representation on Instagram or elsewhere is like a resume for the eyes.

And if you call in sick but then post a photo of yourself having the best time at the Yankees game, be prepared to be fired the next day.

Also, it is okay not to have a social media presence. I think that's healthy and makes me think a person is self-confident, smart with their time, and wise in their approach to life.

This can go a little too far sometimes, though. A colleague at Fox won an award that was to be revealed as a surprise to him. He's never once posted on social media and so we had to use the photo from his ID for the award ceremony. It was a pretty good picture, though, as far as building IDs go!

Here's something I had to do for myself: set time limits on my use of social media. Ask yourself how much time you really need to spend scrolling through dog videos and memes. I love to do that and my sister, Angie, finds the funniest ones, but after fifteen minutes at night, I have to cut myself off. I get lost in it. When I have a moment of "What are you doing?!" I put my phone down where I can't reach it and pick up the novel I want to finish. If I leave my phone right next to my head, I'll succumb to temptation. Not worth it!

WRITING SKILLS MATTER

One of the most shocking things managers find is how few of their new hires can write well. It's a problem. Our education system is failing on this front, so it's important that individuals take it upon themselves to improve their writing.

Why? Well, how you communicate is most of what you'll be doing in any job. Writing clearly and engagingly will help you and your company be more successful. Good writing skills will set you apart from competitors for other jobs, promotions, and raises.

And, it's fun. Once you can write well, you'll enjoy it. There's a reason over three million books get published in America every year. People love to write and to read.

Some ways to improve your writing:

- Read more. I believe my writing improved once I started reading the *Wall Street Journal*, especially the Review and Outlook section, every day it publishes. Find writing you admire, read more of it, and you'll pick it up.

- Get one of these books on writing:

  o *On Writing Well*, by William Zinsser (this is one of my favorites)

- *Dreyer's English*, by Benjamin Dreyer

- *Eats, Shoots & Leaves*, by Lynne Truss

- *This Is the Story of a Happy Marriage*, by Ann Patchett (she describes her writing process and the essays are fantastic)

- *On Writing*, by Stephen King

- Listen to some of these podcasts or classes:

  - Malcolm Gladwell on writing—Master Class

  - *Grammar Girl*

  - *The Writing Room* and *Writers on Writing* (especially if you think you have a work of fiction in you)

CAREER KILLERS: VOCAL FRY AND UP-TALKING

There are a few strange ways of talking, mostly by young people, that may sound cool to some but drives others, especially people you want to work for and impress, absolutely crazy. I'm convinced that speaking this way will hold you back from career success. You will not get the job, promotion, or raise you think you deserve, nor the opportunity to present in front of a client or travel to the company off-site. You'll be stuck.

The most common annoying vocal tics are:

- The vocal fry—where you pretend to have a really deep and croaky voice, like you just woke up after smoking and drinking all night. Far from inspiring confidence in your abilities to communicate, it's pathetic. Cut it out.

- The other is called up-talking—where every sentence ends sounding like a question. As far as I can tell, this starts in middle school when young people aren't assured of what they're saying and so to mask that insecurity, they turn every statement into a question. That way they don't have to take responsibility for anything they say. How can anyone have confidence in you if you sound so meek every time you speak?

- While you're at it, stop saying "like" every other word. I even find myself doing this, especially if I've been around someone who uses "like" as a verbal pause to string together all their thoughts. It's a very distracting way to speak. Observe how every sentence hangs together nicely without "like" weighing it down.

Most of the time these verbal habits develop over time, and people have no idea what they sound like and are surprised when they make terrible first impressions.

The good news is, these habits are easy to break.

I've found that younger staff, when they are privately and gently told they are speaking that way, are genuinely surprised to hear it and grateful for the heads-up. They can immediately stop. It's quite remarkable. But they won't stop unless they're given some guidance, and it's incumbent upon managers and mentors to help them.

DRESS FOR SUCCESS

Keep this advice in mind: dress for the job you *want*, not the job you have.

Workplace wardrobes are much more casual than the *Mad Men* days. Still, you must try to make a good impression. What you wear to work is a part of how you'll succeed.

Your appearance communicates who you are, how seriously you take the job, whether you care about yourself, and if you should be put in front of a client or even be promoted.

»   Avoid: clothes that are too tight, too short, too big, too ratty, heels that are too high to walk in comfortably, and jewelry that is too obnoxious. Oh, and unpolished shoes (the worst).

»   Choose: Comfortable clothes in breathable fabrics that fit well. Classics—black pants and blazer, gray suit, white shirts, simple black dress, good coat. (For more suggestions, just search online—there's a lot of advice out there.)

Is all this cramping your style? Add a bit of color with a belt or scarf, a snazzy tie, but just use good judgment. Dress for compliments, not stares.

Do these rules apply when working remotely? To me they do. If working from home (WFH) is the way of the future, adapt in a way that still says, "Hi, I'm fully present here at work."

Martha MacCallum said that even during Covid when we broadcast shows from our home studios, she would put on her high heels. It made her outfit feel complete and energized for when her program went live.

A young man I know put on a jacket and tie for every morning meeting for his college internship with a crypto company—they met by Zoom as the company was fully WFH—and everyone else was very casual. One intern was even sitting in front of his unmade bed. Guess who made the better impression and got a full-time job offer? Hint—not the messy-bed guy!

But hey, if you're pajamas on the bottom and business up top and you can pull it off without feeling like a slob, I'll allow it.

DANA'S OFFICE PARTY RULES

I'm all for a good time, but there's a time and a place to let loose, and an office party isn't the time or the place.

My number one rule is that you can only have one alcoholic drink at any office event. From the impromptu office happy hour to Fred's retirement party to the annual Christmas bash or Fourth of July picnic. *One.* That's it (and don't pour it into your giant Stanley tumbler).

More than one drink risks you getting tipsy or even drunk and making an inappropriate comment or behaving in a way that your colleagues and superiors—or the staff under your management—will never forget. It just isn't worth it.

You're not a party pooper but you also won't commit a major blooper.

I also recommend making the rounds to exchange pleasantries with as many people as possible. Don't stick with your clique. Use these moments as an opportunity to get to know someone from another department, to compliment a colleague you don't see all the time, and to get to know the people you work with outside of what they do for a living.

Go prepared to ask about your coworker's son's baseball tournament, plans for an upcoming break, or a great new book you're reading that you think they may like. Try to stay focused on the person you're talking to—don't be looking over their shoulder to see if there's someone more interesting or more important who has walked into the room.

Mingle, enjoy, and sip that one drink.

One more thing: do not go to the office party planning to ambush your boss about a promotion or a raise or some other unresolved issue from email.

Or else you might not get invited to the next office party!

STOP, LOOK, AND *LISTEN*

The single greatest skill all great leaders have is the ability to really listen to people.

Listening without distractions can reduce miscommunication and inefficiencies, generate ideas, and make a great impression on those around you.

We all think we can multitask, to write an email or scroll through messages while someone is talking to us. But we really can't. It's not possible to do both well at the same time. Stopping for a moment to look up and listen can make a big difference between mediocrity and success. And if you really must take that call or write that response, excuse yourself. Don't just suddenly ignore someone and get on your phone.

Listening also includes keeping yourself from interrupting others. Sometimes, if a discussion is dragging on, and especially with younger staff, it is tempting to try to cut them off and finish their thought for them so that you can move on. However, do this too many times and it breeds resentment or reluctance to speak up in the future. That's when mistakes can happen that hurt the entire project.

A friend told me that to stop himself from interrupting others, he would casually put his thumb and forefinger in front of his lips and concentrate on what they were saying. That helped prevent him from jumping the gun. His staff respected his attention, and he benefited from getting their unvarnished views.

So set your phone face down on the table. Look at your employees and coworkers and focus on listening. It will serve you well.

MISCOMMUNICATION PREVENTION

Almost all problems in a relationship, a business, a sports team, or any organization are caused by poor communication—either not communicating something or communicating something badly.

There are ways to prevent miscommunication. I'm obsessed with this, and this focus has served me well. Some tips from my experience:

First, think several steps ahead:

- Who needs to know?

- What is the best way to deliver the message—in person or in writing?

- Is your message crystal clear or could it be misinterpreted?

- Spell- and grammar-check your emails, memos, or reports before pressing send.

Challenge yourself to write emails that contain everything someone needs to know in a way that won't lead to any follow-ups. Use clear, direct sentences. Space the text so that it is easy on the eye, with important details bolded or emphasized another way.

Make sure you explain the purpose of the communication, for example:

- This is an update about the plan for the press conference tomorrow morning.

- Here is the information you requested.

- The following is a warning about a concern of which you should be aware.

- ALERT—this is an URGENT message that needs immediate attention.

You should also be direct whether you need something from the recipient:

- This message does not require a response.

- Please acknowledge receipt of this information.

- I will need your reply before 8 a.m. tomorrow.

- Come to my office at noon to discuss.

- Consider signaling what you need in the subject line "Action Required" or "Please Respond by COB (close of business)."

If you're the recipient of a message and you know someone else needs to know about it, first, ask the sender if it is okay for you to forward it to them. Do not forward an email without reading the entire thing. (I once heard of an employee learning he was going to be fired from reading an entire email that was sent to him in error. That was bad for everyone involved.) Let's let that be a lesson for all of us!

Decide also whether the communication should be verbal rather than written. Sometimes it is difficult to insert the correct tone in a written communication, especially a brief text, so decide what is appropriate. A brief conversation can often explain more in less time. Phone calls are not all bad news or confrontations. They can be nice and time-saving.

Find the balance between over- and undersharing. Oversharing can be annoying because you risk people tuning you out. ("Oh no, here she comes again.")

Undersharing risks problems getting worse. "Why didn't you tell me? We could have prevented all of this!" Be the Goldilocks of communication. With practice you'll find the right amount of communication to build you up as a valued asset.

If you use an AI program to generate a first draft, go back through it carefully and make it read like it came from an actual human.

DOS AND DON'TS OF LEAVING A JOB

Most of us will leave a job at some point—perhaps multiple times in our careers—and how you leave can say a lot about you. Here are some dos and don'ts:

DO:

- Be honest and up front about your decision

- Plan ahead for whatever notice you need to give (usually two weeks)

- Have sensitivity for how you communicate with your employer—catch them at the best possible time (so not right before a big presentation for a client)

- Write out how you will tell them so that you have some confidence behind your words.

- Choose to leave with grace and dignity. Understand that your news will not necessarily be cheered by your boss or your colleagues. Remember, most people only always think of themselves first, so when you announce you're leaving, they immediately will think, "Oh no, who will cover your responsibilities? Does that mean the spot is open for me to fill? Are you going to someplace better and for more pay than the current place?" Be prepared to feel disappointed in their reaction and be as kind as possible to them (even if you want to rub it in their faces).

- Leave on a high note. Keep your friends and your contacts. You never know when you may need them some day.

DO NOT:

- Trash the place on the way out the door, either physically or online. There's no need to write a negative post about the company. Karma exists in the working world too, and what goes around definitely comes around.

- Avoid tough conversations about why you decided to leave. Have three main reasons that you can clearly explain so that everyone is on the same page. By doing so, you might help lead to some improvements.

- Give one day's notice. That's rude (unless the situation is abusive or if you are concerned about your safety or a red flag has gone up about the practices of the company).

What if your employer wants to make a counteroffer to get you to stay? You should be prepared for that. Ask yourself, if the money was right and you were going to get promoted or more responsibilities that you were hoping for, would you want to stay? If so, then you can negotiate. But if you want to move on and already have one foot out of the door, politely decline the offer, keep the friendship, and leave with your head held high.

WORK FROM HOME

After the pandemic, many people wanted to continue to work from home (WFH). It's no wonder. WFH provided flexibility to help balance work and family, getting to the Little League game at the first inning instead of the eighth. It meant quiet time and fewer distractions. And less time commuting. It meant you could live where you wanted to live, within reason. What wasn't to love?

Well, WFH started driving the bosses a bit nuts. They need to lead an organization with a common culture to keep everyone together to achieve the company's goals. They were losing touch with their employees, no matter how many video-conference calls were scheduled in a day. And employees were missing out on mentoring, opportunities, and promotions. Many great ideas happen spontaneously in the hallways or on the margins of in-person meetings.

Demands to return to the office went out—and often were unmet. Some people would rather quit than return to the office. Okay, that's one way to deal with it. But there are consequences to performing on a job solely out of your home office.

It is wonderful that there is more flexibility for everyone in today's modern world. We have technology that helps us stay connected wherever we are (also that can stink; see the work-life balance chapter!), yet being at home all the time can affect your performance reviews and future career plans.

Whatever you decide—fully remote, hybrid with two or three days in the office, or fully in the office—accept that your choice has consequences. Be clear-eyed about that. There's no perfect answer here. There's only what's perfect for you currently, consistent with your career goals and family responsibilities. If I may strongly suggest, from a Gen Xer who cares about you, find a mentor or two and make a concerted effort to get advice from them. Keep them posted on your progress, or let them know when you feel stuck. Be respectful of their time, but don't let yourself be too isolated at home. If you're a remote worker, it is your responsibility to keep networking and getting guidance from at least a couple of people you admire.

WORK-LIFE BALANCE PRACTICAL TIPS

- Accept only one weeknight event (this is a great rule that I learned from my CEO).

- Do not feel obligated to explain why you're declining an invitation.

- Think of work-life balance over the course of your life, not necessarily your day-to-day (give yourself some understanding that there will be times when you must work fourteen-hour days; that won't always be the case).

- Block off time on your schedule for exercise.

- Respect other people's time so that you have some balance karma.

- Show up for your friends, even if you have to leave a bit early. This will matter for your relationships and you will almost always walk away feeling that "it was more fun than I thought it would be."

- Never say "no worries" to people who say no to a request—thank them for their consideration instead.

- Consider practicing a ten-minute guided meditation. It's like hitting the reset button of your brain.

HOBBIES

Winston Churchill had a great view of how everyone needed to have something they did outside of work. He said, "The foundation of a hobby and new forms of interest is therefore a policy of first importance to a public man. . . . The seeds must be carefully chosen; they must fall on good ground; they must be sedulously tended. . . . To be happy and really safe, one ought to have at least two or three hobbies, and they must all be real."

He himself became a painter, and he also became a bricklayer—he built the garden walls at his home himself.

When President Bush was thinking about his life in the postpresidency, he considered Churchill's advice. The president already was an avid golfer and mountain biker. But he wanted one more thing that wasn't sports-related. He thought, heck, if Churchill could paint, maybe he could too. So he bought an easel, some canvas, and paints, and hired a teacher. Guess what? He can paint . . . *very well*. He's found joy in that hobby and brought much joy to those he's given paintings to—friends, family, veterans, and immigrants. It's been remarkable to see this talent come through his hands.

When I was in my midforties, I thought about what I could do outside of work. I had my Pilates. And my reading (give me a novel and I'm happy). I had always wanted to learn how to play tennis. A friend bought Peter and me some lessons in South Carolina. I bought all the outfits for my new hobby. And when I tried at first, I was terrible. It was embarrassing. I had a great coach, though, and he had a terrific sense of humor and a ton of patience. Over the years, Peter and I took more lessons together and then I added some solo lessons as well. Eventually I felt good enough to play with other people, and while I'm still not very good, I did get "most improved" the summer of 2024. (It was a private award that the pro only told me about. He might have told every one of his students the same thing!)

So I needed to add one more. What would it be? Well, Peter and I had always wanted to learn how to do a couple of dances so that we could enjoy ourselves more at weddings and parties. I made getting dance lessons a New Year's resolution in 2024. In March of that year, it was still the leftover to-do list item that I kept ignoring. Finally, I said let me just see how this would work.

I posted a note on Thumbtack and immediately got a response from Misha Randalovic and Dakota Pizzi. They're married and together are champion ballroom dancers. I said, "Hey we just need five lessons." He said great, we can do that. Well, a year into it, Peter and I were taking one lesson together a week and then adding one solo lesson for each of us. I enjoy it so much.

We laugh for ninety minutes, and we slowly get better. I love being off my phone during that time, learning a new skill that requires my concentration, meeting people from different walks of life, and working on my posture. I believe this is a hobby we are going to stick with—but I am putting my foot down. I will not compete! (Am I protesting too much? Probably.)

Whatever it is that you think you might want to try, do yourself a favor: Sign up for some lessons. Give it a whirl. If it doesn't work out, you can move on to something else. But find something to add to your life that's outside your daily routine and work schedule.

Now back to the Viennese waltz and the American rumba!

POSTURE

I'm obsessed with good posture—my own, not anyone else's, though I do admire great posture in others! Apparently I'm not the only one. When I searched "tips on posture" I got 109 million hits.

Here's why I'm focused on this:

- At five foot one and fighting a losing battle against gravity, I need every inch of height I can muster.

- Upper-back tightness and soreness caused me endless pain for decades—and cost a ton of money to address.

- Computers and phones are giving us all "tech hump" as we hunch forward for hours a day (who knows what the new virtual reality headsets will do to us).

- Strong posture signifies confidence and leadership to employers, clients, and that girl you want to go up to at the bar.

Dancers have naturally good posture because they've been trained to hold themselves a certain way. We should all take dance lessons as children.

But if you didn't get that chance, what can you do to get better posture today?

- Exercise. I love Pilates, yoga, strength training, and ballroom dance lessons.

- Side sleepers should place a foam pillow between their knees at night. This aligns our hips and prevents imbalances (this was a huge revelation to me).

- Find a virtual posture coach online. There are great suggestions from places like Yogini Melbourne and Tracey Mallet.

- Try an adjustable posture corrector. They make them for men and women.

- Make sure your office setup fits your body and get up every thirty minutes to move and stretch.

- Get a posture buddy, a family member or a trusted friend who will gently remind you to straighten up. You could have a code word for each other, like "Hey-O!" if you want to keep others guessing what you're talking about.

HEALTH AND WELLNESS

Congratulations! You have a part-time job for life: you're the president and CEO of Your Own Health.

In today's world, we can outsource a lot of things we prefer to pay others to do because of time constraints or whatever other reason—dog walking, laundry, cooking, etc.

But the one thing we can't pay anyone to do for us is to take care of our own health. That's solely up to you. It's a commitment you make to yourself and doing so benefits you and the people around you. It is one of the best gifts you can give to your loved ones—to be healthy and mindful of your health (what you can control, of course).

There are plenty of books and websites and Instagram pages about fitness, nutrition, and mental health. We all know about calorie consumption, exercise, and meditation. The industry was over $30 billion in the United States last year. So yeah—we're paying attention.

In my White House years, I did *not* pay attention to my health. At all. I exercised, yes, but I ate very little, drank way too much Diet Coke, slept poorly, and probably didn't take a deep breath for days at a time. I caused myself harm. I developed migraines, a numbness in my right arm from the use of my BlackBerry (yes, a throwback—google it, kids), a ringing in my right ear that didn't even go away in my sleep, and an upper-back ache that could bring me to my knees. I was also snappish with Peter, and that's the worst way to be. I didn't like what I had become or how I felt.

The White House doctor told me it would all go away within six months of the end of President Bush's term. He was fairly accurate on that. But I realize I could have done so much better in my job if I'd been more mindful of my own health. I couldn't ask Peter or my assistant to do that for me. It took a while to unwind from that pace and pressure.

Taking care of your own health is the most important daily responsibility we have. It makes everything else possible.

Today I have a great mix of fitness. I ride my Peloton bike and utilize all parts of the app, including strength and yoga training. I take ballroom dancing lessons (for fun! again, I'm not competing!) and go to Pilates three times a week.

I protect that time on my schedule and only give it up if it's necessary. I pair that with better nutrition and an early bedtime, and I haven't felt this good ever before. But it's a job. I gotta show up to it every day.

It isn't easy, but the most difficult part of any exercise is the first few steps out the door, so keep to it.

Find something that works for you and stick to it. I know everyone says that. Because it's true!

You will be a happier, more productive person if you make a commitment and get healthy and fit, especially if you're a younger person reading this. Get fit in your twenties so you don't have to try to do it in your forties!

CHAPTER 10

Roundup: I Wish Someone Had Told Me . . .

I wish someone had told me not to worry my twenties away because everything turned out okay. As I've gotten older, I realize now what my mentors had been trying to get me to understand, that eventually I'd look back and think, "Wow, I can't believe I wasted so much time worrying about inconsequential matters." There were so many good answers to this question, I put them all in one chapter.

Fill in the blank: I wish someone had told me . . .

MICHELE CHASE

Nobody ever told me that I should check in to see how I'm doing.

Many managers, like pretty much all new parents, really

don't know what they are doing. And they certainly don't like to give bad news or feedback that isn't good.

If you start working for a new boss or even your current one, at some point ask them how it's going. What it does is take what could be an adversarial conversation and make it constructive because you are inviting the feedback.

I ask my CEO on a regular basis, as I have with all of my bosses since I figured this out some years ago, "Is there anything I'm missing? Is there something I should do more of?"

You'll be surprised sometimes by what you hear, and it is most always helpful.

DAN BARR

I learned early on that it is absolutely essential to have the ability and confidence to hire people to work for you who are better and smarter than you.

I learned that if I was the smartest guy on my team or in the room, I was in trouble.

So, I believed my survival hinged on my ability to hire great people and then give them the room and support they needed to make me and the rest of my team look great.

MORA NEILSON

No one really knows what they are doing.

Just because someone has the bigger job, title, status, or power doesn't mean they also don't suffer from imposter syndrome.

They just chose to keep saying *yes* and figured it out along the way.

PATTI CALLAHAN HENRY

To learn to be comfortable with the discomfort of disappointing people.

I am a chronic people-pleaser. My first career was as a pediatric nurse, and I am a mother of three, and caregiving is my go-to default mode. I feel everything very deeply.

Disappointing people or having them be upset with me is unsettling, but focusing on this emotion is crippling to the truth of who I am and what I desire to create and say.

SALENA ZITO

You are never going to make everyone happy and that is a full stop.

DAVID BAHNSEN

I think that, in different moments, I wish I had worked even harder than I did, and in other moments I wish I had unplugged more, been more present.

I don't regret the time I've spent working, but I regret some of the quality of time that I spent with family. There were moments I was physically there but I was still distracted. I wish I had been more consistent in being focused and mentally present with my wife and children all the time.

LAWRENCE JONES

To have a little bit more fun.

FRANCINE LEFRAK

Life's difficulties are all opportunities to learn.

JESSICA TARLOV

Take more risks when you're young.

Trying things—and failing sometimes—helps you find a good fit professionally. Before you're in your thirties you just don't have as many responsibilities, so go for it! Failure is healthy and really not as bad as it looks.

LAUREN FRITTS

Although the hardest days can make you feel discouraged, worried, or even make you want to quit, you will look back on them as the days you learned the most. These tough days are when you expand your skills and sharpen your resolve. They become the stories and examples you share when teaching others.

DR. MARK SHRIME

Very, very, very few decisions—in life, in relationships, in career—are final.

Don't go into your next decision thinking it has to be the rest of your life or you've failed.

That's a recipe for staying stuck.

You aren't on a path. Make the path.

HAROLD FORD JR.

That having kids would enhance and focus my life in ways I couldn't imagine.

I probably would've still waited until I was forty-three, but who knows.

I'm just blessed both of my kids are healthy, funny, smart, and decent.

Amen.

JESSE WATTERS

To eat healthy.

I spent years eating chips, soda, fast food, bacon, egg, and cheeses for breakfast.

Subway sandwiches, chicken tenders, french fries, and processed foods—I didn't realize how unhealthy that was until just a few years ago.

Once I stopped eating that way and started eating whole grains, fresh fruit, vegetables, and nonprocessed meals, I became a much healthier and happier person on the inside and out.

FRANK SILLER

That the depth of sorrow you feel is matched by the capacity for joy you can bring to others through acts of kindness.

BRIAN KILMEADE

Most lessons I had to learn myself—no regrets.

JOHN ROBERTS

To just relax and let life happen. I spent so many years completely stressed-out that I really missed a lot of the joy of just living. Learn the value of humility. Live a humble life. My dear wife, Kyra, drilled that into my head early in our relationship.

PETER MCMAHON

Of the numerous times I've thought "I wish I had known," on reflection most were fairly inconsequential.

And if I had been told something highly significant and potentially life-changing, and taken the relevant action, I would not have been on that flight in 1997 when I sat beside my future wife and my life would have been totally different in every way.

I might have appreciated it at the time, but knowing what I do now, do I really wish someone had told me something a few decades ago?

I don't think so.

JOHNNY JOEY JONES

Experiences with the ones you love last longer than any material object or moment of adulation.

When prioritizing your time and energy, remember who matters most and give them what your job or things will never give you—love.

JEANINE PIRRO

I wish someone had told me to laugh a little more.

PAUL MAURO

I wish someone had told me . . . how much I would miss my father. Whoever you love, appreciate and show them. Because, man, when they're gone, you'll constantly wonder if you did that enough.

I also wish that someone had told me that the best thing in life is this: fun that matters.

Whatever it is that gets you out of bed in the morning—your family, your faith, your work—make sure you are enjoying it at least some of the time (if not most).

We are all, none of us, here for very long. Find the fun. I don't mean "fun" as in bingeing Netflix or videogames or something, but the enjoyment that leaves you, at the end of the day, feeling like you did something worthwhile, that you made some progress, that the world is enhanced by your being in it.

We all know that feeling. Accomplishment plus enjoyment.

That's the real fun. That's fun that matters.

GREG GUTFELD

That drinking was no solution to your problems. That it was the problem masking itself as a solution. And once you remove it from your life, your life becomes much bigger than the delusional relationship you had with substances.

BRET BAIER

Take it easy on the carbs after forty.

PHIL LAGO

I wish someone had told me this will be a long trip with a number of highs and lows. Obstacles that, at the time, appeared to be insurmountable, turned out only to be speed bumps. Enjoy your successes and failures. Learn from them but don't fixate on them.

To be honest, I didn't choose a career path, it chose me. I was an intern at an organization which I had no interest in joining full-time. I needed a summer job, and it was an easy fit. I didn't know what I wanted to be when I grew up, but I was certain this wasn't it. I interacted with some uninspiring supervisors and assignments. But, the head of the 25,000-person organization surprised me with his message about duty, service, honor, and commitment. I had an epiphany and was hooked. I'm not sure if the leader believed his message, but it didn't matter. I did.

STEVE DOOCY

Be nice to everybody.

You never know who that new person is you encounter along the way, and more importantly you only get one chance for a first opinion. Two people I vividly remember from my days at Fox News exemplify that. The first was an overnight videotape assistant on the *Fox & Friends* show who was constantly searching the tape library looking for a video to make great segments. That kid worked terrible hours at probably not-swell pay but had a great attitude.

The other was a college intern during the summer of 2006.

"Hi, I'm Steve Doocy and welcome to the Dawn Patrol," I said to our new intern as we shook hands. "Hello, Mr. Doocy, I'm Daphne."

At that moment the famous political guru Karl Rove popped into the greenroom with a dozen still-warm glazed donuts. I introduced Karl to Daphne and revealed that Karl always brought them in when he was on *Fox & Friends*, and I offered her the first one.

"Thank you, I'm not a big donut person," she said.

"Come on . . . one donut *can't* kill you," I prodded.

"Actually, my dad . . ." she said and then paused.

"*Your dad won't let you have a donut?*" I said with italics in my voice.

As a father of three kids who pretty much were raised at Dairy Queen, I said, "Trust me, your dad won't find out if you have one . . . right?"

"No thanks, Mr. Doocy. Thank you, Mr. Rove."

That's when the stage manager told me to get back into the studio for the next segment.

"Daphne, if you change your mind, the box is right there," I said pointing at the coffee table, "And if you don't eat one, Karl will have to take the box back to the store and ask for a refund!" A few laughs and I was walking out the door.

Out of the greenroom's earshot I said to a nearby producer, "Our new intern says her dad won't let her eat a donut. Who's her dad?"

"Daphne's dad?"

I nodded.

"Dr. Oz."

Oh. What a food faux pas. I almost force-fed a sugar bomb to the daughter of one of the most famous cardiologists in the world.

Had I known she was Dr. Oz's daughter I would not have suggested she try to clog an aorta on her first day on the job. However, this is a good illustration of how you should try to be nice to everybody, even if you don't know who they are.

That is why I *always ask* everybody their name, regardless of who they are or what they do. There are so many people we all encounter daily, it is important not just for identification and clarity purposes, but to be nice to them, to show them you appreciate them.

It can be a lot of people, but we all have a lot of people who share our daily journeys.

At 4 a.m. this morning, a man from Ethiopia named Danny picked me up and drove me to work. Jim the security guy walked me into the building. Hal greeted me from behind the big desk at our world headquarters. Andrew waved me through the turnstile and we briefly discussed the humidity and the upcoming weekend.

Lexi, our assistant, greeted me at 4:35 a.m. and we discussed the previous day's Wordle game. I FaceTimed with producers Rachel and Kristen to discuss the show, then I made some notes. Diego printed them and I was ready to go. Today in the studio our crew was Ed, Ted, Ian, Jon, Chris, Sam, Brian, and Keith. We all play Wordle each day, starting with the same word. Somebody selected HOTEL as our starting word. The solution was FLAKE, and I got it in 5 guesses. There were a lot of 5s and 6s. Some didn't finish. That's what we do during commercials.

At 9:30 a.m., Danny drove me home, then my wife, Kathy, gave me a honey-do list, which consumed a couple of hours. I dropped off dry cleaning with Danny (who went to high school with my daughter Sally) and then I picked up some stuff at the grocery store. Darlene and Lorrie were the checkers today in self-service.

At Market Basket, the gourmet market where my son Peter was a stockboy and daughter Mary was a checker, Dave, one of the managers, went into the back and got me a just-baked Jersey Breakfast Quiche (it has Taylor ham), and Rob the produce guy picked a perfect bunch of basil for a quick batch of pesto.

Don't get me wrong, I encountered a bunch of people who I don't know. I went to a Walmart and knew nobody. But if in my daily routine I encounter somebody more than a few times, I will ask them for a name, and God willing, I'll remember it—and use it, and I know for a fact that they appreciate that I appreciate *them*.

We all have families of blood relatives, then we also have informal groups of people we see and work with every day, who are important parts of our lives. It's important for me to recognize each by name.

As for that young overnight videotape assistant I mentioned earlier, his name is Jay. I never shamed him into eating a glazed donut. I never asked him to pick up my dry cleaning or fetch me an everything bagel with cream cheese. I was always cordial to Jay as he was to me. And that *was a good thing*, because today Jay Wallace is the president and executive editor of Fox News Media. That kid who was on the lowest rung of the TV career ladder twenty-some years ago is now the boss.

Be nice to everybody. You never who that person is—or who they might be in the future.

Acknowledgments

What an honor to be granted an opportunity to put together this book.

It started as an idea I had for Fox News Digital, where I started a series called "Short Questions with Dana Perino." Once a week, I would ask colleagues at Fox News and friends of mine about their favorite childhood games, best restaurant recommendations, and most loved books. It was a hit on the website and social media, so we kept it going.

Over time, I added questions about the best advice they had ever received and how they achieved their goals. There are so many wonderfully talented people who have made the most of opportunities and challenges, and they were generous with their time and advice.

Fox News CEO Suzanne Scott and President Jay Wallace loved the Short Questions series for its scrollable content—and Lauren Petterson, president of talent development, and Jennings Grant, vice president, helped us turn it into a book where all of this great advice is in one place. My longtime editor, Sean Desmond of HarperCollins, called it "a gem," and I'm so glad we could do this together.

My deepest thanks to my assistants and anchor producers, Caroline Sherlund and Kate DePetro. Caroline helped me compile the content, and now she's a young mother raising a beautiful daughter. Kate picked up at the end of the book and made sure it was perfect. Her sunny disposition is an inspiration every day. I am so excited for their exceedingly bright futures.

I want to thank all my colleagues and friends who participated and didn't mind an extra assignment. Fox News, especially *The Five* and *America's Newsroom*, has been a beacon of hope and opportunity for me, and there's nowhere I would rather be than with this team at this time.

And of course, there's my husband, Peter McMahon. There's always been Peter—and thank God for him. He has the best reaction every time I say, "I have an idea . . ."

"Let's hear it," he says. Thank you, Peter.

I wish someone had told me that everything really would be okay—but now I know.

About the Author

DANA PERINO has been with Fox News Channel since 2009. She is a cohost of *The Five*, one of the most popular shows on cable television, as well as a co-anchor of *America's Newsroom with Bill Hemmer and Dana Perino*. She was the first Republican woman to be named White House press secretary and served for over seven years in the administration of George W. Bush, including at the Department of Justice after the terrorist attacks on 9/11. She was the founder of Minute Mentoring after she left the White House.